The Model Manifesto

The Model Manifesto

An A–Z Anti-Exploitation Guide for the Fashion Industry

Leanne Maskell

First published in Great Britain by Practical Inspiration Publishing, 2019

ISBN 978-1-7886-0065-1

Credits for cover image:
Photographer: Rankin
Hair and make-up artist: Jaimee Rose @ UntitledArtistsLondon
Nails: Jessica Thompson @ EighteenManagement
Stylist: Ellie Witt
Necklace and bracelets: Tilly Sveaas
Earrings: Jessie Thomas

Practical Inspiration
PUBLISHING

Contents

Acknowledgements

I AM ETERNALLY grateful to the following people who helped bring this book to life. Thank you to Emmanuel De Lange, Carole White, John Horner and Alison Jones for your time and help in making this book the best it can be.

Thank you to Jennifer Sheppeck, Keith Maskell, Yvette Graham and Jill Graham for your support in my career. To every single person who I may have encountered in either a good or bad experience over the last 13 years while working as a model, thank you – you all contributed to this more than you can possibly know. Finally, to every model who has told me their stories and helped shape the course of this book, thank you for speaking out. The empowerment has just begun.

Acknowledgements

Introduction

IMAGINE THIS: 12-YEAR-OLD Katie is eating a burger with her dad in a restaurant. A man approaches her, asking if she has ever thought of becoming a model. He says that he works for a top London agency and thinks she could make it big, that she could earn thousands of pounds for one day's work and be featured on billboards. He takes her dad's phone number and calls later that evening to arrange a meeting.

Katie's parents drive her to London the next day to meet with the agency, letting her miss school in the excitement. After waiting for one hour, the agency tells them that she could be a great model if she fixed her measurements. Katie doesn't understand what they mean – she has been bullied for being taller than other kids, but not fatter. Her parents are incredibly angry and take her home crying. She develops a severe eating disorder, believing she is fat, and obsesses constantly over the life of glamour she could have if she was thinner.

When she is 18 years old and on a shopping trip in London, a woman approaches her asking if she'd like to become a model. Katie says yes, going to the agency immediately to meet with the bookers. She has her photograph taken in her underwear so that they can see her body. The model agency says that they will represent her if she moves to London as soon as she finishes school to model full-time. Katie has a conditional place at university to study medicine, but she happily cancels her study plans – to the horror of her parents. Filled with excitement, she signs a contract immediately, not understanding a word of what it says.

Katie moves to London, living in a model apartment shared with five other models, organised by the agency. She is given a brand-new portfolio and cards with her pictures on to take to castings, and her parents are satisfied that all is above-board. The agency isn't asking for any money, unlike the fraudulent agencies they had researched online.

Then the work begins. Katie starts receiving emails every evening titled 'Daily Schedule', with a list of addresses for the next day. These are castings, where strangers look at her portfolio and take a card. Sometimes there are queues for hours and she is often asked to undress in front of these strangers, to show them her body or to try on an outfit. On one occasion she is asked to dance, and in another she must kiss a male model while wearing underwear, which is her first ever kiss.

She is also sent on 'test shoots'; too embarrassed to ask what these mean, Katie finds the addresses, which are often private homes, and has her photograph taken. She isn't sure how much she is being paid for the shoots and finds it uncomfortable to be in men's bedrooms while they ask her to undress for photos. However, she wants to model so badly that she decides to do it anyway.

A month later, Katie receives an email titled 'Job'. It lists a time, address and the name of a magazine she has heard of. Katie has watched her flatmates go to jobs and knows they are different from the amateur photoshoots she has been doing; she guesses that this may be a campaign. She replies to the email and asks, for the first time, how much she will be paid. Her agent replies, 'Hey babe, this is an editorial so it's not paid. xx'. Katie is confused and asks how much money she has made so far, with no reply. On the Sunday, she turns up to the job and shoots designer clothes in a real studio, having her make-up done and her hair backcombed into an unusual style; she hardly recognises herself.

Katie visits her agency the next day, which tells her she has to lose a centimetre off her hips before she will be sent on any more castings. They book her a hair appointment at a top salon and ask her to come back in three days to be measured again. To her surprise, her brown hair is dyed platinum blonde. She eats nothing for the next three days, after which her agency tells her she has her first paid job the next day. It is a photoshoot in Turkey, paying £2000, and her flight is that evening. Katie is incredibly excited – £2000! The job is not as glamorous as she expected; the only bit of Turkey she sees is during the airport taxi ride, and she changes 200 times in one day without any breaks, fainting from exhaustion.

Over the course of the next three months, Katie attends hundreds of castings and books five more paid jobs, totalling £2000. She has run out of money to live on, having spent all of her savings, and asks her agency when she will be paid. Her agent tells her that her account is currently in minus, and that she will receive money for future jobs after her debts are repaid. Katie has no idea what they are talking about and calls her parents crying. Her dad finds out that Katie is £2000 in debt to the agency, having 'repaid' £4000 so far. Payment for her hair appointments, test shoots, flights and rent, along with agency commission at 37.5%, has all been automatically deducted from her earnings. He is outraged and threatens legal action, but the agency shows him the signed contract stating that they are permitted to charge expenses in Katie's name. They tell him that Katie is contracted to live in China for the next three months to repay this money and start her career properly.

Why I wrote this book

Katie's fictional story is the daily life of many real, professional models in the UK. Many models have no idea what they are signing up for or of the reality of the industry. They unknowingly sign over their power of attorney to their agency, which can legally sign them into contracts and spend money on their behalf. Not all agencies are as bad as Katie's, but many are.

I started modelling at the age of 13, with my first ever job published in *British Vogue*. I have continued modelling throughout school and while studying law as it has provided me with income and great opportunities; however, I have also experienced and witnessed immense amounts of exploitation. This exploitation should not be part of the job, but it is widely accepted as normal. To be told to lose weight, put on expensive starvation plans, humiliated by strangers, unknowingly having debts racked up in your name, not being paid for months on end or being asked to strip naked at work – this shouldn't be normal behaviour, especially when most models start working before the age of 18.[1]

The more I have learned, the more passionate I have become about passing this insider information on to others, especially those who idealise the industry and negatively compare themselves to fashion models.

Being a successful model is like winning the lottery; regardless of how you look, it is completely down to luck. There is no clearly defined career path and no specific regulation in place to protect models, meaning that thousands of people are exploited on a daily basis in the hope, like Katie, of becoming the next supermodel.

The Model Manifesto has been written to protect the 99% of models that don't make it big – the ones who are treated as disposable objects. It also aims to educate those who wish to be models on how to avoid exploitation, empower themselves and enjoy the benefits of the job.

This isn't a book to help you start modelling. It's a book to bring about change; to stop stories like Katie's being the ugly truth of

---

[1] A report by the Model Alliance cites that 56% of 241 surveyed models began working at age 16 or below; see Model Alliance, '2012 Industry Survey, Industry Analysis'. http://modelalliance.org/industry-analysis

a business obsessed with beauty; to demonstrate how easy it is to fall into a career that is built on exploitation, how this is not something to aspire to. Models are financially, physically, sexually, emotionally and legally exploited on a daily basis, no matter how successful they seem to be.

This book is in an A-to-Z format, covering the modelling industry in general and how best to protect yourself, a bible of everything you need to know to be an empowered, successful model. Each chapter outlines a specific area of the modelling industry and provides helpful anti-exploitation tips to succeed safely in the area.

Starting from the foundations of becoming a model, including why you need a model agency, how to find a legitimate one and busting myths such as 'scouting equals success', we will build on this to learn the real life of a model once they are signed. Navigating unprofessional photoshoots, building a portfolio and figuring out castings are all vitally important parts of becoming a successful model.

The working life of a model requires careful consideration too: how to ensure you will be paid for your work, how to stay safe on jobs (trust me, modelling is a lot more dangerous than it seems) and navigating the world of social media. We will look at understanding contracts, filing tax returns and what to do when your agency asks you to 'tone up' – or live in Asia for three months.

The global modelling industry is largely unregulated and utterly unpredictable, with models being sent across the world at the drop of a hat. A very messy tangle of relationships intertwines between agencies and clients for every single model, often blurring the lines between professional and personal boundaries.

It is more important than ever that models receive the knowledge they need to stay safe and to not only be a successful model, but a smart, empowered one.

'The Model Manifesto' campaign is aimed at targeting the government to change the laws on modelling. You can find more information about this and further resources at www.themodelmanifesto.com.

This book is designed to provide information on the UK modelling industry and no responsibility is taken for the effects of following the advice herein as every situation is different. The content of the book is my own opinion and is not intended to provide any professional advice to rely upon. You are responsible for your own choices, actions and results, and I hope the advice in this book helps you avoid exploitative situations – model or not.

is for Agency

THE MOST IMPORTANT part of your career as a model is having an agency that protects you. An agency finds its models work with reputable clients, negotiates contracts for each job and ensures that it is paid, taking a commission from models' earnings in return.

The agency works for the model – the model doesn't work for the agency. This is something that is often forgotten as many models unwittingly sign incredibly unfair contracts and are heavily taken advantage of by exploitative agencies.

It is very difficult to understand which model agencies are legitimate because there is currently no government regulation monitoring model agencies specifically[2] as models are recognised

---

[2] The Employment Agencies Act 1974. www.legislation.gov.uk/ukpga/1973/35. Model agencies operate under standard Employment Agency regulations and are monitored by the Employment Agency Standards Inspectorate.

as self-employed in the UK.[3] The British Fashion Model Agents Association[4] is accepted as a good guide, with stringent requirements on its members, but its membership list is not exhaustive of all of the legitimate model agencies currently operating in the UK and therefore not fully representative.

In this chapter, I will explain how to recognise a fraudulent model agency, how to join a legitimate one and the relationship that models have with their model agencies. As your agents are the gatekeepers to your work, your relationship with them is very important – which means it can often be used to exploit you.

Did you know?

1. There are no official requirements to start up a model agency or become a model booker.

2. Employment agencies were licensed until 1994, but these were removed with the Deregulation and Contracting Out Act 1994.[5] Today the only employment agencies requiring licensing are those involving agriculture, horticulture, shellfish gathering, forestry, food processing/packaging, nursing and domiciliary care agencies.[6]

3. Legitimate agencies will never require you to pay any money to join them or before finding you work.[7]

4. You don't need a portfolio to join a model agency.

---

[3] UK Government, 'Your rights as an agency worker'. www.gov.uk/agency-workers-your-rights/modelling-agencies

[4] The British Fashion Model Agents Association, formerly the Association of Model Agents, is a trade association of the UK modelling industry. It is officially affiliated with the British Fashion Council. www.bfma.fashion/

[5] Deregulation and Contracting Out Act 1994. www.legislation.gov.uk/ukpga/1994/40/contents

[6] UK Government, 'Employment agencies and businesses'. www.gov.uk/employment-agencies-and-businesses/licences-for-employment-agencies

[7] UK Government, 'Charge fees as an entertainment and modelling agency'. www.gov.uk/entertainment-and-modelling-agencies

5. Many model agency contracts assign the models' power of attorney to their agency, meaning they can act legally and financially on their models' behalf.

How to choose an agency

It is very difficult to work as a professional model even with an agency, let alone without one! Model agencies have expertise within the industry and contacts to promote their models to. They also act as a vital protector of the model – ensuring jobs and clients are legitimate and that the model will be paid. Good agencies will help models strategise their careers and get them work.

A model's first agency will usually be their 'mother agency'. This means that all work a model does has to go via them and they will have the final say on decisions regarding the model. Mother agencies contract their models out to other agencies around the world and earn a portion of their income, no matter where they are working.

There are small, independent mother agencies who don't get a model any jobs but simply contract them out to other agencies. While a few mother agencies may have good relationships with bigger agencies, as they will earn a percentage of the models' earnings for their entire careers, agencies prefer to represent models wholly by themselves. If you are scouted by someone claiming to be a mother agent such as this, it is always advisable to visit legitimate, official model agencies yourself. Otherwise you are giving a complete stranger a measure of control over your life and a portion of your income for doing nothing at all!

In such a sparse, global industry, a model's agent is often a form of identity for them. They become their family, owing to the young age of models and unique nature of the job. It is important to choose the right one for you, because your agency will determine your career.

It is important to first identify the reasons you want to become a model (money? fame? fashion?) and your realistic prospects (it is incredibly hard even if you have all of the requirements, but different areas are more niche than others). You can then research agencies and actively choose your own, rather than 'falling' into the industry and joining the first one that says yes.

A big agency will not always provide a level of supermodel success. Personally, I have always worked better as a 'big fish in a small pond', with smaller, more commercial agencies as opposed to a big pond of top fishes. You will be competing first and foremost against all of the models in your agency – for your agent's attention – and then at castings.

Different agencies have different client relationships, but ultimately all of the relatively successful agencies stand a similar chance of booking work for models. It is now a global market, with clients booking through social media, apps and the internet as opposed to a few limited agencies.

Ultimately it is a free market, and you have to go for the agency that feels right for you, not for what looks like the best. Judge an agency by its reputation, the feel of the bookers and, most importantly, the contract. The contract is the one thing the agency cannot 'gloss over', so it is vitally important to always have a lawyer read it, as can be seen in the chapter 'L is for Legal'.

How to spot a fraudulent agency

With social media, it is easier than ever for aspiring models to fall victim to fraudulent model agencies. There are thousands of agencies operating globally who can access vulnerable children at any time to suggest modelling to them, bamboozling them with false claims and scamming them out of money. Even seemingly legitimate, well-known model agencies can be acting fraudulently, as they undergo no specific checks by the government other than those relating to general employment agencies.[8]

---

[8] The Employment Agencies Act 1974. www.legislation.gov.uk/ukpga/1973/35

The modelling industry is completely different to any other – agencies can tell models how to look, where to live and what jobs to do. Agents have total control due to the expert knowledge they hold at arms' length from their models. Joining an exploitative agency is catastrophic as a result.

The test for whether an agency is exploitative is if there is a transparent relationship between the agency and the model – whether the model is being lied to, either directly or by being deliberately misled.

Signs of a fraudulent model agency may include

- Offers to 'advise you on your potential', 'assess your career' or provide 'a route into modelling'. Describes itself as a 'platform' or 'referral'.
- Charges any model before finding them work, ever. Tells them they need to pay for photoshoots, images, appointments, training, to be on the website or any other services such as hair appointments. An agency is never allowed to charge any upfront fee to a model and can never force anyone into anything.[9]
- Does not give a model a contract upon signing.
- Tells a model they need a portfolio in order to join an agency.
- Pressurises a model to pose partially or fully nude, in underwear or swimwear.
- Offers any money to a model (such as an advance payment) where interest is being charged. They will need a financial licence to do this, the existence of which can easily be checked online.[10]
- Pressures a model to buy images, stating that they will be deleted if not purchased within a short period of time.

---

[9] UK Government, 'Charge fees as an entertainment and modelling agency'. www.gov.uk/entertainment-and-modelling-agencies/fees-for-fashion-and-photographic-models
[10] Financial Services Register. https://register.fca.org.uk/

- Pressures models to spend money on photoshoots to 'build their portfolio' – there will usually be photographers willing to photograph new models for free, called 'test shoots'. Some very good photographers are worth investing in, but these should be the exception.
- Offers to get a model signed with another agency.
- Promises work/high rates of pay – a model often doesn't earn a sustainable income for a long time and work is never, ever guaranteed.
- Has a minimum term that the model must be signed to them before they can terminate the contract at all (seen more in the USA rather than the UK). This could result in a model being unable to leave that agency for several years, whereas the agency would have no obligation to get them jobs!

How to join an agency

Being scouted

Being scouted or 'spotted' means that someone encourages you to do something based on how you look. In modelling, this is usually associated with strangers approaching would-be models and offering them the opportunity to become a model.

You do not have to be scouted to become a model. Ironically, being scouted does not mean that someone will be accepted by that model agency – it is simply an invitation to interview that is usually met with rejection.

Scouting is actually very dangerous, as anyone at all can be a scout, and scouts have a lot of power. Some scouts are employed by particular agencies and some work independently as mother agents. Fraudulent scouts can use their influence to exploit vulnerable people financially and sexually, and can harass them.

If you give someone your details and they see an opportunity to profit from you, they will try their best to convince you to model.

One woman who scouted me told me she may lose her job if I didn't join the agency that she worked for when I had said no!

Being scouted is bizarre – asking someone to do a job simply based on how they look. Would we scout accountants, lawyers or musicians? It is offering someone a ticket to a world they may not want to be a part of and have no knowledge of, steering the course of a stranger's life.

Scouts work absolutely everywhere you can think of – shopping centres, festivals, airports, restaurants, remote towns and villages – they are constantly on the look-out for tall, interesting looking girls and boys. Instagram is often used as an official method of scouting nowadays, which can be dangerous as agency profiles can easily be faked. Fraudulent scouts are known to extort would-be models out of sexual images or money, which has become easier to do than ever while hiding behind a screen.[11]

A legitimate scout will approach you and introduce themselves, telling you that you have potential and giving you a business card if you wish to take the opportunity further. You should always double-check their details by calling the agency's phone number listed on their website and checking that they work there. It is advisable to never give your personal details to a scout.

Thousands of people are scouted and rejected every day, as it is incredibly difficult to join a legitimate model agency. This is especially hard when their hopes have been raised and modelling has been put on their radar, with many people developing negative self-esteem as a result. It is a horrible process to be judged on how you look by strangers and I would advise anyone not to meet with an agency unless they are 100% interested in becoming a model.

As modelling requires serious effort and dedication, models often have to change a lot about their lives in order to become a model,

[11] Sarah Marsh, 'Fake model scouts tricking UK girls into sharing explicit photos', *Guardian*, 6 October 2017. www.theguardian.com/society/2017/oct/06/fake-model-scouts-tricking-uk-girls-into-sharing-explicit-photos

such as where they live or other commitments. It is so important that new models understand this level of dedication and what modelling *really* involves before embarking upon this path, as it is difficult to leave once you start.

Being scouted can be life-changing – it is just up to you to decide whether that is what you want.

Online applications

Most model agencies accept online applications; however, these are rarely successful due to the hundreds that they receive every day.

An agency's website will detail how to apply, usually by a form requesting personal details and uploading images. If an agency is interested, they will invite the applicant to come and meet them, which does not mean that they will be accepted. A legitimate agency will never accept a model without meeting them.

The online application process is dangerous as agency websites can often be faked. A legitimate agency should never ask for money, bank details or pictures of an applicant in their underwear.

'Walk-ins'

'Walk-ins' are how most models end up joining agencies – literally walking into an agency with the hope of being signed. The majority of UK agencies have times listed on their website that aspiring models can walk in to meet them.

Thousands of people walk into model agencies every year, and most of these are met with rejection. It is impossible to summarise what an agency wants from a model, and incredibly difficult to join an agency. While I have been signed to six model agencies in the UK, I have been rejected from at least ten (often while I have been a successful working model). Each time is incredibly demoralising and upsetting. Agencies rarely give feedback and can sometimes be quite rude.

When you walk in to an agency, you do not need a portfolio. The receptionist will decide whether you will be able to meet the bookers based on how you look and, if so, they may come out to meet you, possibly taking photographs (free of charge) and/or your measurements (see 'M is for Measurements'). The bookers may make a decision straight away or ask you to come back for another meeting.

If you are accepted, you may be given a contract to sign which should always be taken away and read over properly as it may be unfair (see 'L is for Legal'). Many models are flustered and excited at the prospect of joining an agency, so may sign without reading a contract at all. It is always good to sleep on this decision and visit other agencies instead of joining the first one that says yes.

An agency may give conditions for signing a model, for example, reaching certain measurements, moving to a new city or leaving other commitments such as university. These conditions may be hard to satisfy – even if they are casually phrased as 'toning up', 'fixing your hair/skin/teeth' or 'focusing on your career', changing your life can be a very difficult, expensive process, not to mention very hard emotionally, especially if it is for somebody else!

Becoming a model can be very fast-paced, with little time for reflection or consideration. Models often throw away great opportunities in the hope of becoming a famous supermodel, which will only happen for the lucky 1%.

Model-booker relationship

Bookers, also referred to as agents, are people who work for a model agency and send models on castings, negotiate their contracts and book them work. Agencies differ; however, generally each model will have an identifiable booker who looks after them, who they can go to with any issues.

Due to the young age of models who may be living alone in foreign cities, bookers often become their entire support network. Their relationship can become unprofessional, with contact outside of working hours.

As bookers are wholly responsible for promoting models to clients, there is a very unbalanced relationship between them and their models. They know a model's entire schedule; whereas models usually find out only the day before about any work they might have, bookers can choose which clients to send the models' images to, can decide if a model is in appropriate shape to go on castings and tell a model to lose weight.

Models must be able to recognise the difference between developing a good relationship with their booker and being exploited – they should never be asked to give money, sexual favours, their free time or anything else in order to work.

Unprofessional bookers may treat some models more favourably than others, invite models out or contact them out of hours and tell clients that certain models are unavailable to work. They may also ask for gifts or money and allow their personal emotions to become involved in their job, which is very dangerous due to the amount of power they hold over models. A sexual relationship should never take place between a model and their booker while they are working at the same agency.

Bookers control their models' entire careers – to upset them is to risk not being able to pay your rent next month. It is very hard to complain about them to another booker or speak out at all, because they may then give you less work! Many model agency contracts require three months' notice for a model to leave, which can result feeling trapped if you are unhappy.

It is important for models to know that they are not helpless. Their booker has a duty to treat them professionally and respectfully, and if a model is unhappy, they are not stuck. They can talk to the head booker and inform their agency about how they feel, and leave if nothing changes. By standing up for yourself, you are showing that you know how you should be treated and respect yourself.

Unprofessional bookers must be weighed up with realism. If you are not working as a model, the best thing to do is speak to your booker about why this is. Sometimes the client feedback will simply not be positive, and there is nothing your booker can do about this. Some models simply work better than others, and it may not be a matter of personal preference.

Generally, your agency will focus on the models they are excited by. If you look amazing when visiting them, have brilliant new images or make an effort to ask about their days, they will be more motivated to book you work. It ultimately comes down to relationships and sometimes these will simply not work out between a model and their agency due to a clash in personalities.

There should be a professional relationship of respect between a model and a booker. It is important for models not to be afraid of their bookers, to visit them weekly and say hello to every booker separately in order to build a strong relationship; however, it is not required for a model to bring them gifts or see them outside of work. Models should treat the agency as work and therefore dress as they would for a casting, arranging appointments with their bookers if they want to discuss something in detail with them.

Models can show professional respect by responding as quickly as possible to any communication, always being reliable and timely for appointments, booking out time they need off in advance and being honest with their bookers. For bookers this is treating their models as human beings, not engaging with their personal lives, organising safe and appropriate work and communicating openly and transparently with their models.

When you have a good professional relationship with your booker, you are able to work much more efficiently. Your mother agency is the foundation of your modelling career upon which the next building block comes – your book.

Anti-exploitation tips

- Never give money to any agency or person related to modelling.

- Never send anyone any compromising images of yourself in underwear (see 'X is for X-Rated') or personal information such as your address or bank details. A legitimate agency will never ask for this until you are officially signed with them and it is for professional reasons.

- A model agency will always want to meet you before signing you and cannot guarantee that you will work.

- Always double-check any details of agencies by calling the number on their official website to verify any employees or addresses.

- Only ever meet model agencies that have a strong reputation (which can be checked online) and only ever at their offices.

- Do not meet with a model agency if you are not 100% sure about modelling and have decided what you want from your own career beforehand. Make sure you explain this to the agency when you meet them, along with any other commitments.

- Remember that being scouted and applying to an agency is often met with rejection.

- Ensure you are a member of Equity, the models' union, who can help in case of issues with your agency. See 'U is for Unionising'.

- Check any model agencies are listed by the British Fashion Model Agents Association.

is for Book

I N ORDER FOR you to start working with your agency, you will need to build a strong portfolio with which to impress clients, often referred to as your 'book'. This process can be exploitative and confusing, involving working informally, for free and in unprofessionally intimate situations often referred to as 'test shoots'. In this chapter, I will demonstrate how to safely build a strong book.

Many people are scammed into paying for unusable images by fraudulent agencies or photographers to become a model,[12] and many professionally signed models are pressured into working for free or paying for 'test shoots' to build their book. These completely unregulated shoots may be with seemingly professional photographers who take advantage of the informal

---

[12] Anna Tims, 'Would-be models duped by "platforms" promising easy route to fashion world', *Guardian*, 18 December 2017. www.theguardian.com/money/2017/dec/18/modelling-agencies-platforms-scam-studio-collective

setting or use these images for their own profit. One thing unites these photoshoots – they all involve exploitation in the hope of booking work.

Did you know?

1. You don't need a portfolio or professional images to join a model agency.

2. Many photographers will shoot models for free (called 'test shoots') – you never have to pay for photoshoots.

3. Newly agency-signed models often work for free in 'testing' mode for several months until they begin earning money.

4. Many test shoots take place in photographer's personal houses, where models are sent alone.

5. Test shoots may be completely unregulated, with no agreed terms, meaning that photographers often believe they own the images, possibly selling compromising images of models years later.

What is a book?

Model agents decide on how a book should look and whether it is 'ready' to present to clients. The images will be on their website and they will usually ask a model whether they want to use an a tablet or traditional hard portfolio. If it is the physical version, the model agency should cover this cost[13] and print out the images in high resolution to place inside the portfolio, which can be impressive but heavy to carry around! Hard books are also less flexible, requiring you to physically print out new images – and a model usually only has one to take to all clients.

---

[13] UK Government, 'Charge fees as an entertainment and modelling agency'. www.gov.uk/entertainment-and-modelling-agencies/fees-for-fashion-and-photographic-models

Using a tablet allows a model to have several different versions of their book to hand, which means they are able to tailor it to the client and boost their chances of success. Agents use their expertise to put together a model's book and know what their clients are looking for, which models can often forget, using the images they like best on a tablet.

Clients will usually be sent a model's book before they even cast with them, as it is viewable online and easy to send via email. If the book the model shows them at the casting is dramatically different, they will look unprofessional. It is always best to be honest with your bookers if you don't like certain images they have chosen for your book and make it a collaborative effort.

I advise using a hard portfolio for important castings and a tablet for the majority – a tablet is also easier to always have to hand in case of last-minute castings. If you don't have one already, this can be a considerable expense so decide yourself whether it is worth it. At present, most agencies aren't buying models tablets!

Composite cards also make up part of a model's portfolio. These are high-quality cards with a model's image, agency details and measurements to give to clients at castings. Model bookers choose the images and give them to their models, replacing them when they run out.

Test shoots

Test shoots are probably the most unregulated area of modelling, which makes them very dangerous. They are how models build their portfolios and gain experience shooting. Sometimes referred to as 'trade for prints', they are usually unpaid and make up a huge part of a model's career, especially when they are starting out. They usually involve amateur photographers who want to build their own portfolios, so models should generally not pay for these images.

However, many aspiring models are manipulated into paying for images, which are rarely usable in their professional portfolios unless the photographer is of professional industry standard. Some very successful professional photographers may charge models for images, but these should be exceptional. The majority of test shoots are unpaid; however, with the importance of social media, photographers that have big followings may charge those who wish to work with them as they may advertise the model to their clients online.

A good policy for test shoots is to never, ever pay a photographer directly. If you really want to work with a particular photographer for the purposes of modelling, you can allow your agency to advance this for you as long as they are not charging you fees. They will take the payment back from the money you earn in the future, but using your agency 'account' can result in a slippery slope of debt, as seen in 'E is for Expenses'.

New models may be testing until their agency feels they are ready to go on castings and with it often taking a few weeks or even months for them to receive images, they may be working for free for a long time. One agency I had hardly used any of the images of the unpaid test shoots they sent me on in my book! Models therefore may be unpaid for months, relying on handouts from their agency to survive, getting them into debt before they have even started working.

Test shoots often lack the usual 'booking agreements' (see 'L is for Legal') applying to paid work, determining how images can be used and who owns them. The agency terms and conditions on their website will usually state that testing images cannot be used commercially; however, this is vague and so leaves the majority of photographers believing and acting as though they own the rights to these images.

Editorials are often called 'tests' because they may be submitted to magazines for publication and so are usually unpaid, where the model is usually working very hard for no money while others profit. Photographers also may sell any images they like at a later date and it is very hard to take action against them if there is no signed paperwork. One model I know saw pictures of herself as a teenager wearing lingerie published in a national newspaper ten years later!

However, test shoots can provide models with great networking opportunities, images and experiences – therefore, some can be very useful. Industry professionals continue to test all the way through their careers, as models do, for their own creative pursuits and to refresh their portfolios, so it can be a very valuable opportunity to work with new people. This should be weighed up against the shoot itself – I have had bizarre test shoots, including being painted wacky colours and having my face completely covered, so the images were of no use to me.

Models are rarely fully briefed before a test shoot, let alone given the option to say no. Shoots can involve literally anyone, from a student to famous photographer, anything from a swimming pool to animals and be located anywhere from a bedroom to a professional studio. A proper lunch is rarely provided and models may be treated badly on test shoots, with no accountable paying client present – often shooting outside, in extreme temperatures, uncomfortable clothes and for much longer than they had been told.

Photographers that have not been properly verified by agencies can be very dangerous. I have been sent to many strange men's houses for test shoots, being incredibly scared and pressured to do things I did not want to do, trapped in a confined location. Models are usually sent to test shoots alone, which is crazy when it is considered that these are often teenagers in the private homes of strangers. There is no standardised policy in place for the protection of models in these situations, unlike other industries where people are vulnerable as a result of working alone, such as the NHS Lone Working Policy.[14]

---

[14] NHS Staff Council, 'Improving safety for lone workers', October 2013. www.nhsemployers.org/~/media/Employers/Documents/Retain%20and%20improve/Managers%20guide_Lc0882_3.pdf

Models can take control of their own portfolios by only working with people they actually want to work with, especially if it is unpaid. You can scout out photographers you want to work with on social media and ask your agency to message them, choosing the type of work you want to invest your time into. Most of your time as a model will be unpaid, so you should treat your time as an investment. Once you have a strong enough book, you will be sent on castings, which are discussed in the next chapter. These are also unpaid!

Anti-exploitation tips

- Never pay a photographer directly for images or be pressured into paying for images you do not feel are a worthy investment. You never have to spend any money in building your book.
- Don't buy a tablet unless you really want to.
- Speak to your agency about your book and strategically plan out how to best build it together, estimating the amount of time it will take for you to start working with paying clients.
- Tell your agency you never want to do a paid test shoot unless it is agreed beforehand with yourself. Avoid using the 'agency account'.
- Ask your agency to only send you to work with photographers that they have personally met and verified, and never to their houses. If possible, ask them to always send you on test shoots with another model.
- Research every test shoot and photographer as soon as you receive the details. Decline to do any shoots in private places (such as hotel rooms!) and always find the photographer's social media profiles to verify their identity.
- Be very careful about what you shoot – testing photographers often believe they can use these images however they like and may try to pressure you to pose in underwear or partially nude. Remember that it is one moment of awkwardness weighed up against a lifetime of worry, and you do not owe anyone anything.

- When you arrive at a test shoot, note all of the exits and if you feel uncomfortable in any way, go straight to the bathroom and call your agency. If you feel unsafe, leave immediately. A good agency will always support you.
- Remember that you can always say no to any shoot, casting or job.

is for Castings

A S A MODEL, you will spend most of your time attending castings. These are modelling auditions, where you will present yourself to a client in the hope of being booked for work. Model castings in the UK are completely unregulated, arranged by a model's booker – which means the model usually has very little information and hardly any control over the situation. The imbalance of power between client and model can lead to very exploitative situations where models can be asked to undress in front of strangers and do things they are uncomfortable with in the hope of being chosen.

In this chapter, I will explain what different castings involve and how to make a positive impression on the client while maintaining your professional boundaries.

Did you know?

1. There are no standard casting policies across the modelling industry and no standardised way of verifying clients are who they claim to be nor standard way that castings should be carried out. Potentially anyone can cast a model if they wish to, regardless of whether they are professional or not.

2. Castings can take place anywhere from hotel rooms to offices, private homes to photography studios. They can involve models being asked to do anything at all, from dancing in their underwear to learning a script. Models rarely have advance notice of what a casting may involve.

3. Models are normally told about their castings the evening before, receiving the time, name and address of the client. They will usually have a few castings per day.

4. Clients can cast as many models as they like, from as many agencies as they want, meaning that queues can sometimes be hours long.

5. Models are not paid to go to castings or for their travel expenses.

What is a casting?

A standard casting involves a model visiting the client, showing them their portfolio, giving them a composite card to keep, possibly trying on clothes and having their photograph taken very informally. Sometimes the client may ask the model to do something else, such as show their personality by dancing or speaking in front of a camera.

Castings can be very physically and emotionally tiring for models, who travel around cities to different appointments and often wait for long periods to be seen for a few minutes. It can be very upsetting if the client treats you rudely or you feel rejected – most models project their own insecurities onto castings, as seen in 'R is for Rejection'.

Usually models are not given feedback on castings, unless they are shortlisted for a job, which is called an 'option'. The client usually confirms which model they want the day before the job. It is rare that they would book a model without casting them first, or at least having seen a video of them, which would be called a 'direct booking'.

Today, clients quite literally have all the models in the world to choose from. It is a global market, and they are no longer limited to even model agencies. I have witnessed the UK's top fashion brands scouting and booking models via Instagram (more on this can be seen in 'I is for Instagram'). In London alone, there are over 10,000 models signed to agencies. Clients can cast potentially thousands of models, so it is hardly surprising that models are so eager to please in such a competitive market.

Models will attend many castings in order to book one job – there is no standard career path to follow. On average, I book 1 out of every 15 castings that I attend, with each casting taking on average around three hours, including travel and waiting time.

Considering this, most models are out of pocket for much of their career – most spend a lot of their time attending castings, with no guarantee of work. Accounting for the months it may take to be paid for each job, many models are extremely financially vulnerable, open to immense exploitation. More information on this can be seen in 'F is for Finance'.

Types of castings

- Request casting: the model has been specifically requested by the client to cast for an upcoming job.
- General casting: there is an upcoming job that a casting call has been put out to model agencies for, so all models fitting certain requirements are sent.

- TVC casting: these are for television commercials, usually requiring a model to show their personality in front of a camera. Models may have to show the way they look from each side (their 'profiles'), their hands and feet and answer some questions or read a script.
- Show casting: this is for a catwalk show or event, so the model may have to show their walk to a client.
- Hair casting: these are usually for hairdressers who will examine the length, thickness and style of a model's hair.
- Go-see: these are when a client just wants to meet a model, to have a good awareness of which models are in town and see their personality.

How can castings be exploitative?

Castings involve models meeting strangers who have immense power over them, with a variety of ways that they can exploited.

Fake castings

I have been sent to several fake castings by model agencies, involving people who are pretending to cast models for a fake job in order to meet with them for other reasons. For me, these reasons have included scouting models for prostitution and escort work, to take compromising photographs and to date models. One such casting was supposedly for a chocolate commercial shooting in the Caribbean taking place in a hotel room, where I was requested to undress to my underwear for photographs, being told that I was too flat-chested for this job but would be suitable for 'event work' in other countries. Models from top agencies were waiting in the foyer to be seen and although I notified them and my agency immediately, there is no way of knowing that other agencies were informed of the dodgy nature of this casting.

As agencies currently do not have a transparent way to verify clients for castings, models place a considerable amount of trust in them, which is why it is vital to be with a legitimate model agency.

Abuses of power

During castings, models are often vulnerable and alone with the client whom they wish to impress, making it easy for them to abuse their power. It is common industry practice for models to be requested to change in front of strangers (with 86.8% of surveyed models being asked to change nude at a casting or job without advance notice[15]) and I have experienced clients speaking to me inappropriately and deliberately humiliating me during castings. I have waited for hours only to be spoken to rudely by groups of strangers, with them filming the entire thing.

As castings can take place anywhere, models may be in places they otherwise would not be, such as the house of a stranger, with no standard processes to ensure their safety, such as a Lone Working Policy.[16] Models are subject to the stranger in question, who could potentially make sexual advances, drug a model or even secretly film the casting to be used as blackmail in the future.

This is not limited to private individuals, as casting agent James Scully[17] demonstrated when he reported the mistreatment of models at a top designer's casting, where models were made to

---

[15] The Model Alliance, '2012 Industry Survey, Industry Analysis'. http://modelalliance.org/industry-analysis

[16] NHS Staff Council, 'Improving safety for lone workers', October 2013. www.nhsemployers.org/~/media/Employers/Documents/Retain%20and%20improve/Managers%20guide_Leo882_3.pdf

[17] Lauren Milligan, 'Supermodels back model mistreatment revelation', *Vogue*, 1 March 2017. Scully is quoted as saying, 'I was very disturbed to hear from a number of girls this morning that yesterday at the Balenciaga casting, Madia and Ramy (serial abusers) held a casting in which they made over 150 girls wait in a stairwell, told them they would have to stay over three hours to be seen and not to leave. In their usual fashion they shut the door went to lunch and turned off the lights to the stairs, leaving every girl with only the lights of their phones to see,' he wrote. 'Not only was this sadistic and cruel it was dangerous and left more than a few of the girls I spoke with traumatised. Most of the girls have asked to have their options for Balenciaga cancelled, as well as Hermés and Elie Saab who they also cast for, because they refuse to be treated like animals.'

wait on the staircase for hours in the dark. Abuse does not have to be sexual – it can be simple degradation.

Castings can sometimes be used as a front for work – sometimes images taken at castings can be used in place of actual photoshoots that a client would normally pay for. Clients can also use them to test whether a model would agree to certain things, such as changes in their hair, not communicating this 'acceptance' to the agency and exploiting a model who does not understand what this change means in reality.

Unrealistic castings

Sometimes models may be sent to castings that they have no real chance of booking, such as a brand casting for a different skin colour to the model or if they are on holiday when the job is taking place. Agencies may do this in the hope that the model will impress the client anyway or change their own plans, which is not only a waste of the model's time, but also the client's. Similarly, clients may cast models at their free will, even if they don't have any jobs coming up.

Practical dangers

As models are often casting in foreign countries, they may not know their way around a city and may be sent to dangerous areas for castings. This requires them to be street-smart – in some countries they may be specifically targeted as models, being highly recognisable (usually tall, lost and confused!). Models also often have their phones out to use their maps, which is dangerous as it leaves them open to being attacked and mugged. More on this can be seen in 'D is for Dangers'.

In some countries such as China, models may be allocated a 'driver' to take them to castings, which they generally have no choice but to pay for. This may mean that their agency is financially profiting from them attending as many castings as possible, as they will pay this money to the agency through future income, as seen in 'E is for Expenses'.

How can models succeed at castings without being exploited?

Ultimately this involves being clever. It's difficult to stand out against the thousands of beautiful models available to the client but easy to impress them with your knowledge and personality – while maintaining your personal boundaries. If you do your research, you can protect yourself against potentially exploitative clients and help your agency to verify which castings are professional and therefore worthy of your time. You will also need to trust your agency completely to have your best interests at heart – if you don't, find a new one.

Models can boost their chances of success by always staying professional themselves. The typical 'casting uniform' for models is tight clothing such as jeans and a vest top to show their body, with heels for females at all castings, with little make-up. It is important for models to always have their portfolio and composite cards with them for castings as this is how the client will remember meeting them.

Models must assess all of the potential dangers of a casting, especially as this represents the potential job. Modelling can be very dangerous as an overall job, as we will see in the next chapter.

Anti-exploitation tips

- Ask your agency to line up your castings with another model. Models from the same agency usually have very similar castings so it is good to have a friend that you can travel with.
- Remember you do not HAVE to go to any castings and can always say no.

- Research the client when you receive your casting and the address, to verify that they are legitimate. If you have any suspicions, speak to your agency.
- Plan out your day the night before, checking how you will travel from casting to casting and how long this will take you. Write all of the casting addresses down on a piece of paper to use instead of your phone.
- Aim to be at every casting 15 minutes early.
- Always listen to directions via your headphones instead of having your phone out on the streets. Never speak to strangers who approach you; confidently walk onwards without making eye contact. Mirrored sunglasses are good for this.
- Assess the risks upon arrival, deciding whether the casting is safe – if anything about it at all makes you feel uncomfortable, call your agency and do not be afraid to leave. If there is an excessive queue, I would advise leaving. Weigh up your time and the likelihood that you will be booked.
- Aim to drop in one professional compliment showing the client that you have researched their brand and are suitable to model for them.
- Inform your agency if you are running late to a casting or cannot make one.
- Make sure that you have full phone battery, a wall charger that you always carry in your bag and a portable charger. Your phone is the most important thing for getting around and keeping in touch with your agency, who may send you last-minute castings throughout the day!
- If a client asks you to change clothes, politely and confidently request a changing area, such as a bathroom. If they ask you to undress you should have had prior warning from your agency and do not have to undress at all if you do not feel comfortable. Simply state that you would prefer not to – a professional client will never demand this of you.
- If a client requests to photograph you at a casting, assess this properly – could the image realistically be used to sell the

clothes/on social media? Do you feel comfortable? If not, tell the client.

- Don't pay for any 'casting/walking training' – this is not required and an agency will always train you for free if they feel you need it. It may be advisable for models to attend a few acting/confidence/self-defence courses to improve their overall confidence in castings.

- Converse with the client (such as asking what they are casting for) but do not give any of your personal information, such as your address or phone number. Avoid speaking to a client directly outside of a professional setting such as a casting, and inform your agency if they ask you for any personal information.

- If a client is treating you in a way that makes you feel uncomfortable, say, 'you are making me feel uncomfortable'. Always tell your agency as soon as possible.

- Remember that you do not have to honour anything you say in a casting, as your agency will refine the terms of a contract prior to the job. However, be honest with the client about what you are comfortable with in order to maintain professionalism.

- When in a new location, always make sure you know where your country's embassy is and have emergency money at your accommodation.

- Use apps that share your location with your family, especially if you are working abroad.

- Do not let your possessions out of your sight at castings, for example, in queues while you go in to meet the client.

is for Dangers

MODELLING IS RARELY as simple as just having your picture taken – it can be very hard, dangerous work, involving anything from posing on an elephant on the streets of India to walking down a runway in eight-inch heels. Blindfolded.

Due to their lack of official protection, models must be able to recognise and identify potential dangers in order to protect themselves.

In this chapter, I will explain the different dangers that may arise for models during the course of their work and how to avoid them.

Did you know?

1. There is no standard job in modelling – work can involve anything at all, from standing in the same pose for five hours to underwater photoshoots.

2. Many contracts state that models retain full legal liability, despite allocating their legal power of attorney to their model agency. This means they can be sued by a client if they breach the contract, for example, by not turning up to work – even if they were not told about the job!

3. Most models rarely see the contracts for their individual jobs or these do not exist at all due to informal arrangements. This means that they may have no idea of their legal rights or responsibilities.

4. Most models are not covered by insurance and many are injured during the course of their work, with no compensation.

Potential dangers at work

*   Dangerous working conditions on set may involve abandoned, unsafe buildings, dangerous props such as motorbikes, working with animals and working in unsafe countries. Your agency should be informed of any risks and check that you feel comfortable, in full knowledge of what is expected from you, before booking the job.
*   Models can catch diseases and other illnesses from dirty equipment, such as skin diseases from unwashed make-up brushes and even head lice from hairbrushes.
*   Many models suffer burns while at work, for example, by hairstylists using hot irons carelessly, dangerous props such as motorbikes and excessive sun exposure on a job!
*   Hairstylists, clothes stylists and make-up artists can easily hurt a model if they are unprofessional. For example, models can have their hair torn out by backcombing or their eyeballs poked by make-up artists.
*   Dangerous products such as poor-quality make-up, hair dye or body paint may be used on a model.
*   Models can be advised to undergo practices such as regular sun bed use or taking dangerous medication to lose weight by an exploitative agency, which negatively impacts their health in the long term.

- Models may have an allergic reaction to certain make-up or hair dye, so it's important that they know of any allergies they may have.

- Models may become exhausted on jobs with unrealistic expectations, such as shooting 200 outfits in one day. They may be denied breaks and sufficient water/food. Models rarely take time off work, are constantly travelling and may have unhealthy diets, which means they are at high risk of exhaustion.

- Models may be expected to shoot in extreme weather conditions, usually in completely inappropriate clothes, such as shooting fur coats in 40 degrees or bikinis in snow.

- Clothes themselves may be dangerous, such as excessively high heels or highly flammable dresses. Many models have broken bones or fallen off the catwalk during shows as a result of dangerous shoes. Clients also often expect models to wear shoes that are too small or too big for them on a job, causing injury to their feet.

- Models may often encounter danger on the streets, especially abroad. They are very open to attack, naturally drawing a lot of attention to themselves.

- Many models are subject to very dangerous situations abroad as they are under the control of the client, with the potential to be attacked, kidnapped or trafficked.

- With exposure to drugs, alcohol and smoking (76.5% of surveyed models have been exposed to drugs and/or alcohol at work[18]), some models become addicted to a very dangerous, unhealthy lifestyle that can kill them. See 'S is for Sexual Exploitation' for more.

- Various dangerous situations may arise for models, such as being expected to sleep in the same bed as a stranger on a job or being stranded at an airport in the middle of the night.

---

[18] The Model Alliance, '2012 Industry Survey, Industry Analysis'. http://modelalliance.org/industry-analysis; 56% of 241 surveyed models began working age 16 or below.

- Models may not have proper visas to be legally working on various jobs if they do not know they need them. They are wholly responsible for this, and working illegally can result in them being arrested or banned from countries for several years. More on this can be seen in 'V is for Visas'.
- Models may unknowingly break certain laws because of advice given to them, such as to accept cash payments from foreign work and laundering this through airport security, which can result in them being imprisoned.
- As seen in 'T is for Tax', models may be subject to fines if they are unaware of the obligation to file self-assessment tax returns, as there are various myths surrounding tax for models and many do not even know they are self-employed.
- As seen in 'O is for Overseas', foreign agency contracts can be problematic, especially if they are for a certain amount of money, where if models wish to leave they would have to repay this money to the agency! Often, their passports are taken upon arrival and they must abide by various rules such as not being sunburnt or having certain measurements to not break this contract – of course resulting in them being vulnerable.
- Models may be pressured into shooting nude or wearing clothes they do not feel comfortable wearing, such as lingerie. Compromising images may be used to blackmail them in the future, as seen in 'X is for X-Rated'.
- Abuse may arise in situations where models are especially vulnerable, as seen in 'S is for Sexual Exploitation'.

Anti-exploitation tips

- Obtain insurance to legally protect yourself in case of issues arising at work. Equity offers models £10m public liability insurance and accident insurance, including £10,000 in case of facial disfigurement[19] as part of their subscription fees, as seen in 'U is for Unionising'.

- Ask to see a 'booking agreement' for every job you are booked on in order to know what is expected of you. See 'L is for Legal'.
- Know that you can always leave a job. Speak to your agency as soon as possible if you ever have an issue at work. Engage in a risk assessment before going to any job by researching the team and address online, particularly if it is abroad. If you ever feel uncomfortable, clearly state this on the job.
- Always feel confident to check whether professionals have properly cleaned their equipment. More on this can be seen in 'Q is for Questions'.
- Take your own make-up/brushes to jobs if you have sensitive skin and do not be afraid to speak up if you feel uncomfortable about anything at all on a job.
- Ensure that you and your agency have always given full, informed consent to any physical changes a client wishes to make on the way you look.
- Ensure a skin test has always been done well in advance of any chemicals such as hair dye being used on you.
- Know of any existing allergies you may have and ensure your agency passes this information on to any clients.
- Never harm your long-term health for modelling – avoid taking medication you do not need or engaging in unhealthy dieting to lose weight.
- Always request suitable provisions to keep you healthy and safe, such as a heater if you are shooting in excessively cold conditions, or regular breaks.
- Ensure your street safety by undertaking self-defence classes, wearing mirrored sunglasses to avoid eye contact, having a rape alarm on your keyring and avoiding using your phone in public.

[19] Equity Models Network. www.equity.org.uk/getting-involved/networks/models-network/

- Avoid any addictive substances at all, including alcohol, drugs and cigarettes. If you are ever offered these at work, decline and inform your agency.
- If your agency ever requires you to go abroad, ensure you have a valid working visa.
- Ensure you are registered as self-employed in the UK and file regular tax returns. See 'T is for Tax'.
- Inform your agency that you never wish to use your 'agency account' and request that they never expense anything on your behalf, as in 'E is for Expenses'.
- Never allow someone to take images of you that you feel uncomfortable with and if you are ever blackmailed, go to the police immediately. Remember that images you take will exist forever, so carefully consider what you may want to do in the future and how modelling may affect that.

Models are exposed to danger largely as a result of their severe financial vulnerability, where they can become severely indebted to their model agencies as a result of being charged for expenses 'on their account'. As we will see in the next chapter, agencies may charge interest rates with models not even knowing what they are being charged for until they see it on their statements, needing more money as a loan to live on as their job payments automatically repay these debts. This results in models being desperate to work and earn money and less likely to stand up for themselves in dangerous situations.

is for Expenses

ONE OF THE biggest myths surrounding the modelling industry is that you need to spend money in order to model. Although this is definitely not true, thousands of aspiring and professional models are financially exploited every day in the name of 'expenses'.

It is shockingly easy for even a very successful model to be in serious debt to their agency. I have experienced pressure to incur agency debt all the way through my career, with some agencies refusing to explain how their system worked and treating me negatively when I enquired about it.

Models may find it hard to identify what expenses are and question their agency about them due to the imbalance of power, lack of information and utter lack of accountability. This isn't even to mention those who are exploited by people instructing them to spend money in order to join an agency in the first place!

In this very important chapter, I will demystify modelling expenses, explaining how debts can occur and how to protect yourself.

Did you know?

1. Models never have to spend any money in order to join an agency, build a portfolio or start work.

2. Model agencies can spend money on behalf of their models, with the legal power of attorney assigned to them in most model contracts. The money is repaid when the model starts earning money, automatically deducted from their income.

3. Agencies do not always tell models about these expenses in advance. They also do not have to provide invoices or receipts for these, so there may be no proof of payment.

4. In the UK, agencies must adhere to the law of what can be charged to a model.[20] They generally cannot charge for anything prior to finding a model work.

5. If a model agency wants to charge a model any money, such as interest rates on advance payments, they will need a financial licence, which can be checked online.[21]

Personal expenses

Personal expenses regarding modelling are those spent by the model themselves, directly out of their own money.

These may often occur when con-artists deliberately mislead models and instruct them to spend money themselves on different expenses such as photoshoots. Fraudulent agencies operate in this way, to exploit aspiring models in particular out

---

[20] UK Government, 'Charge fees as an entertainment and modelling agency'. www.gov.uk/entertainment-and-modelling-agencies/fees-for-fashion-and-photographic-models

[21] Financial Services Register. https://register.fca.org.uk/

of as much money as possible, informing them that this is the required investment they need to get started, with no intention of finding them real, paid work. Often this involves networks of people who are taking a cut of any money that a model pays out, such as an agency and photographer being financially connected.

However, professional models may indirectly invest into their own careers and these costs theoretically may be legitimate – but remember that none of them should ever be necessarily required in order to become a model. See 'T is for Tax' to assess whether these expenses may be deductible from your overall income for tax purposes. If a modelling agency pays for any of these expenses, always ask them to send you a receipt.

Agency expenses

Agency expenses occur when a model agency pays money on behalf of a model; they can deduct this from the model's future earnings as a debt to be repaid. This can include money paid to a model that isn't directly from the client, essentially a loan – even potentially incurring interest fees that the model may be unaware of.

Some agencies may act as unregulated banks, spending and lending money without any receipts, credit checks or permissions. Models often wait months to be paid for work, and borrow money in order to cover their living costs – resulting in a constant cycle of debt that they cannot escape. They will never be in a positive balance and this is in their agency's interest. If they are in debt, they are trapped and may be forced to pay this back to the agency – which prevents them from leaving the industry. Despite agency expenses practices being certainly unethical and legally questionable at times, it is usually enough for an agency to simply scare a model.

Models will have an 'account' with their agency that acts as their virtual credit account. If expenses are placed 'on account', this means that they will be deducted from any money earned by the model, as the agency receives it from the client.

This process can be very hard to keep track of and agents do not always inform the model as they charge these expenses, so models may find out by seeing them on their financial statements months later. I have been charged for many things without any knowledge at all until I see my statement, at which point I have felt far too embarrassed to 'make a fuss' for something that happened months ago.

A model will generally have to repay any outstanding debt if they wish to leave an agency; however, this is not always chased in reality as many models don't have the money. Some agencies can contractually take up to three months to pay a model, so they may be without income for a very long time, even when they start working. Agencies are legally required to pay their models within ten working days of receipt of any of their money from a client[22]; however, this is very hard to prove and some contracts exclude this.

Due to the complete lack of financial transparency and communication, many models are terrible at understanding their own expenses, statements and finances – leaving them wide open to financial exploitation. Exploitative agencies can directly profit from this lack of knowledge.

Potential modelling expenses

In the UK, general practice is that model agency commission should cover all marketing costs of the model incurred in-house, such as website fees.[23] Remember that if you are ever charged for any expenses, this should be explained to you beforehand, with your express written consent and a receipt provided afterwards.

---

[22] The Conduct of Employment Agencies and Employment Business Regulations 2003. www.legislation.gov.uk/uksi/2003/3319/pdfs/uksi_20033319_en.pdf

[23] UK Government, 'Charge fees as an entertainment and modelling agency'. www.gov.uk/entertainment-and-modelling-agencies/fees-for-fashion-and-photographic-models

In other countries, it is very common for agencies to charge marketing costs to their models' accounts. Explained below are also many other expenses often associated with modelling that you may see on your 'account' as a model.

Marketing fees

These should not be charged in the UK; however, foreign agencies may charge models for the following expenses.

- Portfolios. Models may be charged for the hard portfolio folder and the professional printed-out images that go into this. As seen in 'B is for Book', many models use a tablet as their portfolio, the cost of which is not currently covered by most agencies.
- Composite cards. Printed on high-quality card, these are replaced by the agency whenever they run out.
- Courier/messenger/Fed-Ex fees. Prior to the internet, portfolios were once physically couriered around cities and models were charged for these transport fees. Some are still charged these today.
- Website fees. Many agencies charge models for featuring on their website.
- Show package. Models may be charged to appear in a Fashion Week 'package' sent out to clients, often with specific composite cards printed due to the large number of castings they will attend.
- Social media/digital marketing fees. These fees are for a model's promotion on the agency's social media accounts. Most agencies hire someone to specifically manage their social media.
- Administrative fees. These may relate to the cost of running the model agency.

Other expenses

These may appear on a model's account or be paid for directly by themselves. I have always tried to avoid using an agency account so always mainly covered these costs out of my own pocket.

- Travel. If a model is booked on a job outside of their city it is typical practice for the client to cover their travel costs, which requires a receipt to be sent to the agency by the model in order to expense this back. However, if a model is not travelling for a specific booked job, or sometimes even if they are, they may be paying for the travel themselves. If an agency claims to cover flights or books them without your permission, it is very likely that they will be expensing this back – nothing is for free. See 'O is for Overseas' for more.
- Rent. Models may be instructed to live in other cities for a few months at a time. This requires short-term leaseholds, or for them to stay in model apartments, which are usually agency-owned accommodation leased to models on a nightly basis. Models often mistakenly believe this rent is for free and don't ask how much they are being charged to live in model apartments, which are notoriously bad value and quality, as seen in 'O is for Overseas'.
- Hairdressers' fees. Agencies may tell their model how to maintain the condition and style of their hair, referring them to specific hairdressers. I was sent to a hairdresser costing me around £400 – they dyed my hair brown, which I absolutely hated!
- Gym/personal trainer/nutritionist/dermatologist fees. Models may be referred to certain professionals regarding how their body and skin looks, usually specifically advised to them by their agency. I know of some models who had to pay £30 per day for a daily 'detox food delivery' when their measurements weren't right – an expensive diet!
- Clothes. Models may be advised to dress a certain way for castings. I had one agency literally take me shopping and pick out the clothes I should wear!

- Test shoots. As seen in 'B is for Book', some models may pay for test shoots to build their portfolio, but they should always know about this and make an informed decision beforehand. I have been charged for test shoots without even knowing until I saw my statement months later!
- Visas. Models are legally and financially responsible for their own working visas. Foreign agencies may sometimes cover their working visa on their 'account' there, as can be seen in 'V is for Visas'.
- Pocket money/advances. Agencies often may give models cash as an advance on particular jobs they have done or 'pocket money' (weekly or monthly allowances) if they cannot cover their living costs. The agency will normally not give out cash advances for free, charging interest on any money given – in the UK they need a financial licence to do this.[24] This is often seen for models working overseas who do not have easy access to a bank account and can quickly lead to huge debts.
- Spray tans/waxes/grooming. Models may be required to undergo grooming procedures such as regular spray tans to maintain their overall image, which they will pay for unless a specific client covers this for a job.
- Language lessons. If a model is living in a new country for a period of time, they may be advised to take language lessons.
- Training/lessons. Legitimate agencies do not usually require their models to pay for training; however, some may choose to attend classes such as acting courses in order to improve their chances of booking work.

Staying on top of your expenses will help you manage your finances more generally, which, as we will see in the next chapter, is critically important for models to fully understand. Financial exploitation is one of the main ways that models are exploited.

---

[24] Financial Services Register. https://register.fca.org.uk/

Anti-exploitation tips

- Be very cautious of agents who pressurise you to use your agency account or call it 'investment' – it is debt, most likely intended to trap you with that agency. You never, ever have to accept an expense – either covered by your agency or yourself.
- Ask the agency accountant to explain their account system to you upon joining any new agency. Clearly state to them in an email that you do not wish your account to ever be used unless they have your express permission beforehand and that you require a receipt for the charge.
- Always question your agency about any expenses on your statement that you weren't told about in advance. They often 'forget' and may make mistakes, charging you incorrectly.
- Always look for other options whenever an expense is proposed to you – your agency may have a special relationship with the person being referred by them that is benefitting them. Sometimes this can be helpful if the referral will give discounted rates, but occasionally they may be directly profiting off the agency and their advice may not be needed!
- Check if and when your agency charges an advance fee and if they are licensed to do this.
- NEVER start borrowing money from your agency for personal reasons such as to purchase a car (which I have seen happen)! If you have literally no other choice but to survive on advance payments, try to keep these for your minimum survival needs.
- Not all expenses related to modelling are deductible from your income for tax purposes, as seen in 'T is for Tax'. Write all of your jobs and castings in an excel document and note all of your expenses related to them.
- Never rely solely on modelling for income – always have a part-time job. Advice on this can be seen in 'Y is for Your Career'.
- Never pay anything in order to join an agency.

- Take a photo of all receipts and keep them on a virtual folder on your phone. Always send any receipts incurred on a job, such as lunch or train receipts, to your agency to claim back from the client for you.
- Do not be afraid to leave an agency because of your debt to them, which can quickly spiral out of control and tends to get worse rather than better. Equity can help with this, as seen in 'U is for Unionising'.

is for Finance

A S A MODEL, you never know when your next payment is coming. It is so hard to book any job, let alone a well-paid one, that figuring out how to financially survive becomes very difficult. Models rarely see their contracts for individual jobs and often have no idea how much or when they are being paid.

It is hardly surprising that models are incredibly exploited financially due to this lack of transparency. That models earn high incomes is probably one of the biggest and most laughable myths of the industry – 99% of models are grateful to receive anything they can get, and have to make this money last until their next payment. It's rare that models can properly survive off modelling alone, leaving them extremely vulnerable.

Finances are impossible to predict for models – whereas one model may not work at all during a month, another may work every day. If a model is lucky enough to secure regular clients and books a few very-well-paid jobs, they can be catapulted to the other end of the spectrum and earn a very high amount of money in a very short amount of time.

Aspiring models must have a realistic understanding of their potential income, as modelling is difficult to leave once you have started. The chances of earning seemingly high income compared to working for minimum wage, the glamour compared to a nine-to-five and the unpredictability of the job keeps models hooked. Not to mention the debt that models may unknowingly owe to their agency, which prevents them from leaving until this is repaid. Did someone say modern-day slavery?

In this chapter, I will explain how to fully understand your finances as a model and give advice on securing financially stability in an unstable world.

Did you know?

1. There are no legally enforceable, standardised rates of pay for models. They are often expected to work for free or for products, even for world-famous brands.

2. The majority of model agencies take commission from models (around 20–25%) and charge the client a fee (around 20%) for every job.

3. Most models never see their individual job contracts detailing the breakdown of commission and total payment charged to the client.

4. On average, models are paid around three months after completing a job. This can often be even longer – I once waited a year to be paid.

5. No tax is paid on behalf of the model in the UK – they are self-employed and must file a self-assessment tax return at the end of each financial year.

How models can be financially exploited

If models don't see or understand their contract for individual jobs, they have no idea how much they are owed or the terms of payment. This means the agency can deduct any amount of the payment it likes from the total sum for each job, which is very dangerous if it is not operating truthfully, as models have no way of checking this. As they usually give their power of attorney to their agency, which signs on their behalf, models often don't even know these contracts exist, let alone see them.

This also means that money owed to models can be held in others' bank accounts, accumulating interest. Due to the lack of accountability and transparency, models may have no idea when clients have paid and do not know that this money is being protected in client bank accounts on their behalf.

By educating yourself on the below facts, you can equip yourself against financial exploitation as a model.

Financial transparency: the facts

Agency payment processes

- Agency payment systems should be explained to the model upon joining and they should be introduced to the agency accountant, providing them with their bank details. Sometimes models may have to email to check whether any money has come in for them in order to be paid – it is not always automatically passed on.
- A legitimate agency should tell their models how much they are being paid when they are sent the details for a job; however, some do not tell them this or only include the rate without the agency fee. There is no standard practice so models should request in writing to see the booking agreement for

any job and to know how much money they will receive after commission.

- By law, agencies must pay models within ten working days of receiving payments on their behalf.[25] This obligation is sometimes excluded in agency contracts.
- Models should regularly receive a financial statement detailing their jobs, outstanding and completed payments and any expenses charged to them. Agencies may spend money on a model's behalf (often without informing them in advance) and loan money to models. For more on this, see 'E is for Expenses'.
- If a client does not pay a model within the time stipulated in the contract, the model agency may take them to court to receive this money. The legal fees may be charged back to the model – every agency operates differently.
- Agencies hold models' money in a 'client (model) account',[26] which means their money should be protected in case of bankruptcy. As a member of Equity, models can receive free legal support in cases of non-payment. See 'U is for Unionising'.

Agency commissions

- In the UK, model agencies are not permitted to charge both the model and a client commission.[27] Therefore, many legitimate agencies invoice the client a gross sum to pay, including the agency fee.

---

[25] The Conduct of Employment Agencies and Employment Business Regulations 2003. www.legislation.gov.uk/uksi/2003/3319/pdfs/uksi_20033319_en.pdf

[26] UK Government, 'Record keeping for employment agencies and businesses'. www.gov.uk/record-keeping-for-employment-agencies-and-businesses/records-about-workseekers

[27] UK Government, 'Charge fees as an entertainment and modelling agency'. www.gov.uk/entertainment-and-modelling-agencies/fees-for-fashion-and-photographic-models

- The model fee is deducted before a model receives their money, usually around 25%. This can be adjusted based on the model.
- In total, an average model agency receives around 37.5% of the gross invoice inclusive of agency and model fee.
- UK models are self-employed and have to pay their own tax at the end of the year – the agency does not pay any of it. They receive no holiday or sick pay, nor maternity/paternity leave. See 'T is for Tax'.
- Usually clients pay VAT for booking models; however, models may pay this if they are VAT-registered, which should be discussed with an accountant.

By educating yourself and equipping yourself with knowledge, you can ensure that you are financially stable and much more difficult to exploit as a result. This leaves you free to enjoy all of the positive things about modelling – of which there are many, as we will see in the next chapter.

Anti-exploitation tips

- Whenever you start working with a new agency, make an appointment with the accountant and ask them to take you through everything you need to know. Ask questions such as how much commission they take and what their payment procedures are. Ensure they always tell you how much you are being paid for every job that you do and that they send you a monthly statement.
- Ask your agency to send you the 'booking agreement' for every job that you do, detailing the usage and terms of payment.
- Find an industry-specialised accountant for each country you are living in. Your agency will be able to refer you to one – this is vital to ensure you are aware of the tax obligations in that country.
- Record all of your castings, expenses and jobs on a spreadsheet and update it when you are paid to keep track of payments.

List reminders for payments every time you book a job for however many contractual days your agency states it will take to pay you (which can be found in their contract). By having reminders on your calendar, you will be able to chase these payments, which is especially helpful for work with foreign agencies that may have been done a long time ago.

- Always ask your agency about what the length of usage for a particular job is and list a reminder in your calendar for a week after it expires. Check if your work is still being used – if so, inform your agency to chase additional payments. Remember to always check in with previous agencies on whether they have received money from clients on your behalf for jobs that may have been 'bought out'.

- Have your agency pay your money into a savings account, where you can remove a basic monthly 'salary' for yourself to live on regardless of how much you have made that month.

- Have another source of income to cover these costs so that you can be financially secure, such as retail work.

- Save at least 30% of your income in a savings account for tax purposes.

- Ensure that you always know your bank account details from a foreign payment perspective (e.g., your SWIFT code) and pass this information on to any new agency that you work with.

- Avoid spending money frivolously – it is easy to spend and hard to earn! Even when you are working well, you can go out of fashion with clients at any time.

- If you are not paid by your agency after a certain period of time, email the accountant every week to ask if the money has been paid. If they ignore your emails, telephone them. If you still have an issue, go in to see them. Equity can assist its members with non-paying agencies, or you may be able to take them to the Small Claims Court. If the client is refusing to pay, your agency may take them to court – it is important to be fully aware if they choose to do this and check if they are charging you for any legal fees.

is for Gratitude

IN ORDER TO maintain the determination needed to succeed and equip yourself against potential exploitation as a model, it is important to always have a positive outlook on the industry, despite its flaws. By remembering what your motivations are for working as a model, you can enjoy the amazing, once-in-a-lifetime experiences that modelling offers.

As the majority of models fall into the industry by chance, with little knowledge of what it involves, they may not really consider whether they will enjoy the job. When you are facing so much exploitation, it can be difficult to remember the good things – which is why in this chapter, I will discuss all of the wonderful opportunities modelling can provide and advise on how to maintain gratitude in your daily life. This will enable you to actively choose your career every day and empower yourself to focus on the good.

Did you know?

1. Models can be paid thousands of pounds to enjoy incredible experiences, such as shooting in an exotic location with all expenses paid by the client.

2. Models are able to work with the world's top designers and creative talents, gaining an insight into a range of businesses and seeing the most exclusive new fashion collections each season.

3. Models can potentially survive on one day of work per month and enjoy a lot of free time to pursue their other interests.

4. Every day is completely different for a model, which makes for a very fast-paced and exciting life.

5. Being self-employed is amazing if you can protect yourself and truly be in control of your career – you are essentially your own boss.

Advantages of modelling

- Inspiration. From next season's couture gowns to being part of the design process, a model is constantly surrounded by art, creativity and talent.
- Free time. Due to the instability of work, models enjoy a lot of free time during which they can pursue their other interests and passions.
- Flexibility. Modelling can be a very flexible job, fitting around other commitments such as university and internships.
- Working with highly successful, talented people. Models can learn a great deal from those who they work with, which can lead to other career opportunities. More on this can be seen in 'N is for Networking'.
- Travel. Models are able to travel the world, sometimes for free. They can be booked on a job shooting in the Caribbean

at a moment's notice or live in Australia for three months. Modelling is a global job, where the world is your oyster.

- It's fun. Modelling itself can be very fun – from playing dress-up in beautiful clothes to acting out scenes with professional actors. My favourite jobs involved acting with a dog and shooting wedding dresses in the Maldives!
- Unique experiences. Modelling is a truly once-in-a-lifetime job, where you can see your face on a bus or find yourself having your photograph taken underwater. Nothing is off-limits, which can be dangerous (see 'D is for Dangers') but also very exciting and memorable.
- The unpredictability of the job. Not knowing what you will be doing in a week can be exciting or stressful depending on how you look at it. You can book a job paying hundreds of thousands of pounds or you could be sent across the world on a moment's notice – modelling is an extremely fast-paced, exciting job.
- The potential to earn a high income. Although many models are extremely financially vulnerable and do not earn high incomes, some jobs may pay very high rates, especially compared to other jobs such as retail work. It is very common for models to earn £1000 for one day of work, which makes up for the instability of work. If you are sensible and can save this money, you could buy a house or start your own business.
- Being your own boss. As models are self-employed, they learn skills that will equip them for running their own businesses in the future and can be empowered to run their own lives and careers. See 'Y is for Your Career' for more on this.

Despite the brilliant opportunities that modelling can bring, success as a model is like winning the lottery – it is a result of genetics and luck, not a solid career path. There is no promotion at the end of it if you work hard enough, nor any guarantee of working at all.

Possibly because of this limited time frame and opportunity for success, it is important to enjoy the moment and be grateful for every positive thing modelling can provide right now. Acknowledging that you are extremely lucky allows you to realistically reflect on your career and make the most of it. There are several ways to do this, which I discuss in 'Z is for Zen', but my favourite is writing down what I am grateful for every day.

By equipping yourself with a positive, realistic outlook on the industry, you can empower yourself as a strong model, avoid exploitation, say no to things that do not serve you and be in control of your own life. We will see more on how to do this in the next chapter, covering decisions that only you should be making about your body.

is for Hair and Skin Care

MODELS MUST ALWAYS have clean, healthy hair and skin to succeed in their work. This can be difficult when they are being constantly abused by heat, backcombing and heavy make-up at work!

In this chapter, I will discuss the problems that may arise, how to protect your hair and skin as a model and how to empower yourself to ultimately choose how you look, instead of allowing others to decide this for you.

Did you know?

1. Models can be contractually obliged to follow their agency's instructions on how they should look, from their hair colour to the clothes they wear.

2. Some models I know have been instructed to take dangerous prescription drugs in order to maintain good skin.

3. Models must tell their agency if they want to change their appearance, such as getting a tattoo or hair change.

4. If a model dramatically changes the way they look, such as a hair colour change, they will have to reshoot their entire portfolio.

5. Models may have their hair severely damaged or changed on a job in a way that they did not agree to, with no compensation.

Hair

A model's hair is a huge part of their career and overall identity.

Agencies often instruct models on how their hair should look. A good agency should take into account how you want to look – you will never be confident if you don't like how you look! While one forced me to have brown hair, other agencies did not require me to do this.

On jobs, a hairstylist will style a model's hair according to the client's requirements – the model does not have a say. Models may have their hair burned, backcombed or bleached on a daily basis – they are at the mercy of the hairstylist of that day. Hairstylists rarely take the time to help models after the job is over. I have often been spotted pulling gigantic backcombed knots out of my hair on the tube home!

There are many jobs with hairdresser clients who style, cut or colour models' hair. Generally, they will not be able to change how a model looks without first confirming it with the agency. As the jobs are often highly paid, models may be tempted or pressured to undergo dramatic changes without properly considering the consequences – or the hairstylist may not stick to their word! It is quite hard to define 'a trim' or a 'colour refresh' over email. Hair jobs may leave models having to reshoot their entire portfolio and being unable to work with their regular clients, as their hair may be completely destroyed. Many models I know have had their hair bleached beyond repair or cut in ways they or their agency did not agree to and were unable to work as a result.

Body hair

Male and female models often don't understand what amount of body hair is appropriate for work, mainly because there is no status quo, it is something we rarely discuss in society and it is such a personal thing.

If a model is called up for an underwear job that day and they are unprepared then they may feel very awkward if they have excess pubic, leg, chest, armpit, back or facial hair if it affects the job. It can lead to a model having personal body hair removed by a stranger while on a job, which can be very intrusive!

Agencies should educate their models on how clients expect them to be prepared in terms of this, especially for young, self-conscious models who may hurt themselves in the process of trying to be perfect – I once shaved my arms, which was a big mistake! Models should always have any hair removal procedures done professionally. The general expectation is to have as smooth a body as possible.

Skin

Models are generally expected to have perfect, clear skin. This is unrealistic as everyone gets spots – especially teenage models who are going through puberty. They may be kept from attending castings until their skin clears up or referred to a dermatologist, which can be very stressful and expensive, causing more spots!

The best way to maintain clear skin is by drinking lots of water, eating healthy food and avoiding alcohol and cigarettes. By developing a daily skincare routine including exfoliating and moisturising with good-quality products, models can ensure their skin is kept in good condition – always remembering to remove any make-up applied on jobs as soon as possible.

Models must protect their skin fiercely – they can easily contract diseases from unwashed make-up brushes or wear a lot of make-up for jobs. They should always tell the make-up artist of any allergies, check that brushes are clean and that the make-up is of good quality. A respectful make-up artist will usually ask a model if they want to curl their own eyelashes, which I would always recommend as I know of a model whose eyelashes were sliced off by a make-up artist in this way!

General maintenance

- Models are usually advised to keep out of the sun by agencies so that they do not damage their skin and avoid tan lines. It is helpful to wear strapless swimwear and high-SPF lotion while on holiday.

- If you are advised to be tanned, you should be given the option of having a spray tan and never encouraged to use a sun bed.

- Models are allowed to have wrinkles – all humans do, and they can be edited out if needed. Botox is not a requirement and models can work all the way through their lives.

- Plastic surgery is generally not celebrated in the industry and I recommend avoiding it. I know of some models who have been pressured into undergoing plastic surgery by their agency, which should never happen.

- If a model has tattoos, noticeable scars or piercings, they will usually tell their agency upon signing, who should ensure that clients are aware. Normally, models are preferred to have clean skin, with one piercing per ear. However, having tattoos and piercings does not mean a model cannot work.

- If a model has any visible cuts, burns, bruises or injuries they should always tell their agency as if they turn up to work with significantly visible injuries the job may have to be cancelled or the client may try to not pay them. Usually clients can airbrush these out, but it is always better to be upfront.

- Models are also expected to have straight, white teeth. Some are encouraged to have whitening, but this is a personal choice and can be done by natural remedies such as coconut oil pulling instead. Good dental hygiene is vital.

- Nails are expected to be clean, healthy and natural on jobs. It is advisable to avoid any synthetic products such as acrylic nails, as these can be hard for make-up artists to remove on set.
- Models are always expected to be clean when turning up to jobs – with clean, dry hair and freshly moisturised skin.

Models should equip themselves with this information so they do not turn up to a job unprepared or encounter serious injury at work. It will also help them to maintain their personal boundaries and stay professional, which aids in booking more work in the future. As we will see in the next chapter, today there are several other professional methods that models can use to boost their chances of success.

Anti-exploitation tips

- Speak out if you feel uncomfortable with anything at all regarding the way someone is treating you. If you don't like a suggestion of what will be done with your hair, say this as soon as it is suggested. By being confident and self-assured, you can make your own decisions about how you should look.
- Be respectful to those you are working with by preparing the best you can for jobs, turning up with clean skin, hair and nails. More on this can be seen in 'K is for Knowing What to Expect'.
- Ensure you have a skin test for any hair dye or other chemical products that will be used on you for a job 24 hours beforehand.
- Do not be afraid to ask hairstylists and make-up artists about their hygiene. More on this can be seen in 'Q is for Questions'.
- Use a good heat protection spray and skin moisturiser before arriving at a job.
- Take your own hairbrush or make-up brushes to a job if you wish to, especially if you have sensitive skin.

- Decide what your own personal wishes are regarding how you look and inform your agency. If you feel uncomfortable discussing private body hair, you can request not to be put forward for jobs where this could be an issue.
- Establish a routine every few weeks to maintain good condition of your hair and skin. Avoid 'at-home' treatments such as home dyes!
- Never take any dangerous medication that has not been prescribed by an independent doctor.
- Avoid make-up and applying heat to your hair when you are not at work to give it a break.

is for Instagram

INSTAGRAM HAS COMPLETELY changed the modelling industry. Giving models a voice, it has become a virtual extension of their portfolios, showcasing their personality far better than a two-minute casting ever could. Instagram has also opened the floodgates between clients and models, reducing the need for an agency – they can easily contact each other online. This can be problematic if models are not knowledgable or confident enough to properly negotiate their own work and if clients are not who they claim to be – legitimate agents do a very important job of protecting their models, as seen in 'A is for Agency'.

Instagram has introduced a whole new sector of diverse models for brands, which is very hard to figure out as these influencers, models and non-models alike, can be approached directly for work. Instead of having an agency ensure they will be paid and (supposedly) check out the client, they can take their careers into their own hands and book their own work. However, it is important to remember that essentially this is literally speaking to strangers online. Brands are easily able to manipulate people into working for free or for products, where they would normally have to pay a model thousands of pounds. Essentially, Instagram has opened up the market to a whole different competitive playing field, and rates have dropped as a result.

As Instagram has become such an important part of modelling (with clients often preferring to use it over a model's portfolio), I will explain how to master the social media world and navigate yourself safely. You don't need to be Instagram-famous to succeed, but simply show your authentic personality and use it as a marketing platform for yourself.

Did you know?

1. Clients will often view a model's Instagram account before booking them, with many models' usernames appearing on their composite cards and agency websites.

2. 'Influencer models' are becoming more and more prominent now, with some agencies having entire divisions for models with high followings.

3. Models are commonly asked at castings how many followers they have, with their agency portfolios featuring their Instagram handle. As followers relate to potential sales, many clients prefer to use models with high followings.

4. Many top companies are scouting and booking models off Instagram nowadays.

5. Clients can profit from Instagram images in a brand-new, unprecedented way that agencies struggle to price properly. Programmes such as Instagram Shopping[28] mean that they

---

[28] Mary Beech, EVP and Chief Marketing Officer of Kate Spade New York, 'reacting positively to the new shopping experience, which allows [the customer] to seamlessly tap and shop the product – going from inspiration to information to purchase in just a few steps'; see 'A better shopping experience on Instagram', Instagram Business Blog, 21 March 2017. https://business.instagram.com/blog/a-better-shopping-experience-on-instagram?locale=en_GB

are profiting more than ever from models' work, whereas models are being paid less.

Managing Instagram as a model

Building an authentic, strong Instagram following is notoriously difficult. It has become a huge part of daily life, an extension of our personalities to show our highlights reel to the world.

Models already suffer with separating their identity from being a model. They are being viewed by clients but also by their peers, and Instagram does not work in quite the same way as it does for their friends. Their model agency might tell them off for posting a picture of them eating pizza, blurring the lines between having a private life and a job, interacting with people as friends and as clients. It raises the ultimate question: how do we define modelling work?

As a model, you are essentially running your own business and need to market yourself in any way that you can. The best way to do this online is to create healthy, professional boundaries, by having two Instagram accounts – one public and one private. The former can show your public persona and personal brand, always considering clients and the image you want to portray to them. Having a private account allows you to maintain privacy and a separation from work.

It is also important for models to view Instagram as a business in order to be able to psychologically disconnect from it and take measures to be mindful about their social media use. As seen in 'Z is for Zen', Instagram can negatively impact our health and self-esteem, which models tend to already not have a great deal of!

Instagram as a business

Instagram can be incredibly empowering – it can give you a solid base from which to launch businesses, advertise yourself to clients and use your voice. It is great for connecting with and researching teams before modelling jobs and even potentially providing a platform to book your own work, not to mention building your digital skills.

By firstly establishing how to build a strong, healthy presence on Instagram using the advice below, you can then prepare yourself against the unprecedented potential for exploitation.

- Identify your brand. Think about what makes you *you* – what are you passionate about? Authenticity is key – if you stay true to yourself, others will follow.
- Understand your aesthetic, which is how your overall Instagram account will look – build a colour scheme and stay consistent.
- Create a routine. For models, I advise posting every one to two days, at the same time, when your audience is most engaged. By setting your Instagram to 'business' mode, you can view where your audience is based and the best time for posting. Try to stay off Instagram other than this scheduled time, especially for the first and last hour of your day.
- Once you have figured out what you want to use your voice for, incorporate it into how you look. Your beauty as a model is part of what makes you *you*, and this is what clients want to see. This can be done by filming videos of yourself, photographing yourself doing your passions or incorporating your brand into the captions of your modelling work.
- Use your voice by speaking honestly about how you feel and don't be afraid to be vulnerable. It is much more appealing to brands to see a model that stands for something, rather than a blank, beautiful face.
- Film videos. Instagram TV is a great way to record videos showing your personality, and can result in clients booking you without a casting! Instagram stories are also an amazing way to engage with others and show a little 'behind the scenes' of your life and work. Have a 'highlights' reel of some basic casting videos that clients can easily view.

- By incorporating your passions with your modelling work, there are limitless opportunities for collaborations. Follow people with similar brands to yours and connect with them by commenting on their images. By posting about each other you can 'share' followers.

- The quickest way I have found to grow followers is to host competitions. This can be quite hard if you don't have a product or big following already to promote to, so you can partner up with businesses and come up with giveaway competitions.

- You can write comments underneath your pictures with hash tags and geo-tag the location, so that more people can find you.

- Create your own content. Shoots are as easy as asking a stranger to take a photograph of you, and this is also an extremely valuable CV skill.

- Create your own opportunities for work. Comment on client's profiles, drop them a message and ensure that they notice you. Instagram is a great way of being able to contact your favourite clients directly – although it is very important to stay safe and ensure you are not breaking any agency contracts by working outside of them. It is always best to refer clients to your agency, who can demand higher rates and ensure you are paid.

- Stay up-to-date. Every time you see a new social media app, get on it and start creating!

- Engage with your followers by always replying to messages and comments, and interacting with others on their profiles. Treat them as real conversations.

- Remember to keep your Instagram professional, and never post anything that may harm your reputation such as drinking alcohol. Avoid posting personal things on your public account unless it is part of your overall brand.

- Accept your agency's advice on Instagram – they often hire social media specialists to train their models, which can be very helpful. Ask them for help, such as filming video content for your Instagram.

- Don't feature something that you don't believe in, even if you are paid to do so – it will affect your overall brand.
- Remember to always tag everyone involved in a shoot when you post a picture from work and acknowledge their value in every post that you do.
- Unfollow anyone that makes you feel unhappy and remember not to let Instagram take over your life.

Anti-exploitation tips

As Instagram is such a new world, it is even less regulated than the traditional modelling industry! It has opened up the floodgates for virtually anyone to become a model, with various models being exploited by unscrupulous clients and making very dangerous mistakes. By following the below advice, models can protect themselves online.

- Remember that people speaking to you via Instagram are strangers and may not be who they claim to be, even if they have an impressive Instagram. Followers can easily be purchased to seem legitimate. Be extremely careful when speaking online to anyone you do not know in real life.
- NEVER send any compromising images to anyone online, especially those in your underwear, swimwear or nude. See 'A is for Agency', which explains how a legitimate agency will never ask for images such as this. They can be used to blackmail you in the future.
- If a client messages you to work directly, refer them to your agency. If you do not have one, ask another adult to check out the client to ensure they are legitimate. I highly advise avoiding meeting anyone who messages you on Instagram unless you know them in person or know people in person who have worked with them before.
- Be careful of what you agree to on Instagram. Social media work and shoots for Instagram likely fall under model agency

contracts, which is something many models do not realise. I have got into trouble with my agency for agreeing to receive clothes for a social media shoot, because it meant I had undervalued myself and set a lower rate for the industry in general.

- If a client wants you to post a photo on your own profile, they are asking for your social media services. If they are asking you to 'collaborate', this usually means working for free! If they want you to take an image of yourself in clothes and post this, it means you are producing the shoot, modelling and editing – saving them a lot of money!
- Assess your own value – I would advise charging £100 per post for every 10,000 followers that you have. If you particularly like a brand and are happy to receive products or social media promotion in return for your services, be aware of lowering your overall commercial value and remember that the images can be used however they like.
- Remember this when posting your work images on your account – view each post as a virtual currency. You are providing advertising space on your Instagram account to whatever you choose to post about, and some clients may benefit hugely from this promotion. If they ask you to post a picture from a job, always inform your agency, who will charge money for this.
- If you are charging money for a service and do not have a model agency, ensure that you establish this in (electronic) writing with the client. Ask them to confirm the rate of pay, what exactly they want from you (e.g., number of posts/ images) and the time within which they will pay you. This is your informal contract! Remember that it will be much harder to obtain payment or products from companies based abroad.
- You may have to send the client an invoice via email in order to be paid. It is very easy to find an invoice template online, but remember to include your bank account details so that the client can pay you. Remember to state how long they have to pay – a normal amount of time is 30 days. If they do not

pay you, you may be able to take them to the Small Claims Court if they are based in the UK.[29]

- Avoid posting images involving highly sexualised lingerie, nudity, smoking or alcohol.
- You are legally required[30] to state in the caption of an image if you are paid to promote something. This can be done by a simple hashtag of 'ad' or 'sponsored'.
- Remember to include any income from social media in your tax return at the end of the year – it is income! See 'T is for Tax'.

Digital marketing

You can market yourself online in a variety of ways that will indirectly boost your Instagram following. These can include the following.

- Facebook. Create a Facebook business page in your name to promote yourself to the people you know, who will then promote you to the people they know. Facebook networks tend to be more personally engaged – some models have become viral by posting about their experiences on Facebook, which have been shared by others on their profiles, launching their careers. Facebook is great for 'shock value' statuses that can be shared.
- Youtube. This has become a huge industry in itself, and is a great way to share your passion with others, use your voice and build skills in video creation. Audiences tend to be very engaged and there is potential to earn money from advertising.
- Twitter. Featuring mainly text updates, this is a great way to easily connect with others, form opinions and use your voice.

---

[29] UK Government, 'Make a court claim for money'. www.gov.uk/make-court-claim-for-money

[30] CAP, CMA, 'An influencer's guide to making clear that ads are ads', Advertising Standards Agency website. www.asa.org.uk/uploads/assets/uploaded/3af39c72-76e1-4a59-b2b47e81a034cd1d.pdf

- Pinterest. This is often used by brands for inspiration when organising photoshoots, so it's advisable as a model to set up an account and keep an updated portfolio on Pinterest, with relevant hashtags so clients can find you.
- Blog. This is a great way to show your interests, writing and website skills. You can also feature your modelling portfolio images – I blend my latest photoshoots into my blog posts. Website design is very easy, with websites such as Wordpress and Squarespace doing all of the hard work for you. Blogs can also lead to other opportunities – this book was supposed to be a blog post!
- Online forums. Many of these exist where fans of fashion and models discuss the latest trends. One way models can put themselves on the map is by posting their work there – by building up traction on a forum they will direct interested people to their Instagram.

Mastering your marketing will allow you to reach clients and show why they should book you for work. In the next chapter we will explore the many different kinds of jobs that fall under the umbrella of modelling work!

is for Jobs

ONE OF THE best things about being a model is the range in jobs – no day is the same and by fully understanding this you can choose your own career instead of having it decided for you. In this chapter, I will give a thorough explanation of everything you need to know, including the different rates of pay and requirements for different types of work.

As it is so hard to become a model, models often join whichever agency accepts them first and work in the sector they are allocated to without questioning what this means. Different agencies focus on different types of work and it is important that a model finds the right fit for them. It is hard to understand what the different types of jobs and genres involve if you aren't experienced in the industry and, as I learned, they dramatically differ from each other and can offer completely different types of careers.

Being a model is similar to being an athlete – there are several different sports and athletes need to know which one they are best suited to and most passionate about in order to succeed. They can then choose how much dedication and effort to give this – at an amateur, casual, full-time or premier level. If a model ultimately doesn't want to do the job or doesn't know what it is, there is no point in them trying to do it.

I spent years figuring out the different types of jobs while doing them, building up experience of what I did and didn't enjoy and what I wanted from my own career. Using the advice in this chapter, you can do the same – without having to go the long way around and be exploited on the way.

Did you know?

1. There are many types of jobs within modelling that all pay completely differently.

2. High-fashion modelling is known to pay less than commercial modelling, with some top magazines paying models nothing at all to feature in them. Contrastingly, some online retailers may pay models £1000 per day to model for them!

3. Certain types of models will have different physical requirements – women generally have set height and measurements, whereas men normally have to be over a certain height to model.

4. You can choose the type of model you want to be, within reason. Different agencies focus on certain genres of modelling and by researching the sectors you can work as a team with your agency to best strategise your career.

5. Models are not usually told what different jobs or genres of modelling involve when they're starting out.

High-fashion/image modelling

High fashion is an area of modelling that is highly esteemed and involves a lot of hard work and dedication. The jobs are often not very well paid due to the prestige involved, but can be very creative

– with models bringing to life exclusive designer collections and appearing in magazines and fashion shows. High-fashion models often are very tall, thin and unusual looking, with females around 5'11" and size six to eight, and males over 5'11".

Editorial photoshoots

Editorial jobs involve models having their photograph taken to be published in a magazine. These jobs are often very badly paid – ranging from nothing at all for the majority of shoots to around £250 per day. Print editorial is largely moving online these days, with many photoshoots being submitted to magazines in the hope of being featured. Models can use these images in their portfolios and get to wear next season's trends.

Editorial photoshoots can take place anywhere and involve anything at all. They tend to be very creative, bringing to life a 'story', involving bizarre concepts such as posing with animals or shooting in extreme conditions such as a desert – ultimately, editorials are supposed to inspire and shock. Models should always be properly told about what these shoots involve (they are often given no prior warning) and be given a real choice to decline work.

Editorial photoshoots can potentially lead to much bigger campaigns that are very highly paid, but it is important that a model is doing professional editorial shoots and not wasting their time. Often, the more successful the magazine, ironically the less you will be paid – this goes for covers too!

Test shoots

Test shoots will make up a huge part of any model's career, as they are images that models shoot to build their portfolio, as seen in 'B is for Book'. High-fashion models in particular shoot many test shoots throughout their careers to gain a range of imagery. These are usually unpaid for everyone involved, so that they can use the images to build their books.

Sometimes agencies or photographers may try to convince models to pay for test shoots, which I would advise strongly against as most people will be happy to shoot for free with a professional model. A legitimate agency will always build a model's portfolio free of charge.

Test shoots can take place anywhere at all, often taking place very informally with amateur photographers, which can be dangerous for models if they are treated unprofessionally.

Models often test a lot at the beginning of their careers to build their portfolios, which is a good way to network with industry professionals who are also constantly updating their portfolios. If you are charged for a test shoot, this should not exceed £500. Typically, a professional photographer would charge between £100–300 for a test shoot with a professional model, but it is best to avoid these unless you feel it is a very worthy investment.

Look-books

High-fashion models may model clothes for a client's physical booklet they use to sell their clothes, mainly to fashion buyers and specific customers. They are similar to e-commerce jobs, with lots of changes and simple poses; however, they are more 'one-off' days than regular work. Rates can range between £500 and £2000 per day.

Runway

High-fashion runway shows typically involve a catwalk, where models walk up and down a platform modelling clothes to an audience. Runway shows are very prestigious and are often a mark of success for high-fashion models; however, they are not very well paid. In my experience, most runway shows pay from £50 to £1000 per day.

Although fashion shows may occur year-round, Fashion Week is usually the most important time for runway models, with many agencies using the shows to present models to top global designers. This usually involves a month of shows around the world with the top designers of each country showing their collections, with models travelling from country to country to attend castings and fittings for the shows a few days later – essentially competing against the world's top models. Haute couture shows are also very highly esteemed, with models showcasing incredibly expensive, custom-made clothes.

Runway shows generally involve 5–20 other models having their hair and make-up done for a few hours, before walking down the catwalk for 30 seconds each. It always amazes me how much work goes in to them and how quickly it's all over. See 'W is for Walk'.

Fittings, showrooms and presentations

Runway models may do this kind of work during off-peak show seasons, acting as the mannequins on which the show-pieces are created. Fittings are where the clothes are made on the model by a designing team and showrooms are when the clothes are shown to buyers on the model, who will try clothes on at request. There are showroom seasons, where models travel to different countries with designers to model their clothes to international buyers, normally divided into autumn and spring collections.

Presentations are mini-shows where clothes are presented to many buyers or customers at one time, often with models standing completely still. These can also take place during Fashion Week – I have done many and stood still for hours, with people coming up to me like I was an animal in the zoo. They are generally paid less than shows, despite requiring much harder work!

This work can be tiring but is regular, paid work for models (around £50–200 per hour, usually booked for a few hours at a time) as designers may use one or two models per season. It requires very precise, consistent measurements and a quiet, patient model.

Commercial modelling

Commercial modelling involves work that actively sells something to an audience. It makes up a huge proportion of the current fashion market, as online fashion brands are so successful and fast-paced.

Whereas commercial work was once roughly limited to catalogue and campaign work, it is now an enormous industry embodying everything from e-commerce modelling to commercial catwalk shows. The work tends to be very well paid and requirements are less strict for models, with different heights and body types accepted.

Today, models can easily be both high-fashion and commercial models, as there is such a blend between the two sectors. Some model agencies may focus solely on commercial modelling, with strong links to clients and understanding the ever-changing demand for diverse models in this industry.

Generally, commercial models do not have to fit into the strict requirements of a high-fashion model – females are usually around a size eight to ten and 5'8" and above, whereas men can be over 5'9". Commercial modelling also embodies several niche sectors such as plus-size modelling and is becoming more inclusive every day.

E-commerce

E-commerce can be an excellent way to make a lot of money if a model succeeds with big online retailers. This work currently makes up most of the market in the UK, with some brands shooting up to 24 models every day, each changing between 30 and 150 times! Rates vary between £300 and £3000 per day depending on the brand and how well a model is selling for them, which companies can work out by an algorithm.

The downside is that it can be hard to enter that market, and it can be quite mind-numbing work. A far cry from glamorous shoots on the beach, this will be very monotonous work, doing simple front/back/side poses all day. However, models are usually very well treated, as they are usually working for big companies with good employment standards, provided with lunches and breaks.

E-commerce models should study the poses on the website and be sure to show their personality to succeed. Days can be long and quite boring, and the client wants models who can bring fun into those days.

Commercial editorials

These are fashion spreads in commercial magazines and newspapers. They may involve more high-street fashion as opposed to designer clothes and are often better paid than typical high-fashion editorials, at around £300 per shoot.

Commercial shows

Many companies that are not exclusive high-fashion designers have fashion shows, which can range from enormously prestigious underwear catwalks to jewellery presentations. These shows may be viewed as more 'happy' than high-fashion shows, with models walking down a runway smiling and wearing high-street clothes rather than next season's exclusive collection. They may be paid more than Fashion Week shows due to the more commercial aspect, in my experience paying around £400–1000 per show.

Catalogues

Catalogues are physical booklets featuring a brand's clothes to sell to their customers, often produced on a mass scale as advertising rather than focused on individual, specialised sales, as a lookbook tends to be. Catalogue shoots may take a few days and are typically very well paid, in my experience over £1000 per day. Models are traditionally happy and healthy, smiling in the pictures to appeal to as wide an audience as possible.

Campaigns

A campaign involves a model fronting a brand for that season's collection. Campaigns can be featured online, in shops, on buses or trains and pretty much anywhere else you can think of. Each one is different, and some can be shot in studios while others can be shot abroad in amazing locations.

They are usually known for paying extremely well; however, they are incredibly hard to book. They can be 'bought out' for a lot of money for many years after doing the initial job. Beauty and perfume campaigns are often the most highly paid, potentially paying hundreds of thousands of pounds, depending on the model. Most campaigns start at £500.

Television commercials

Usually referred to as 'TVCs', these jobs may be incredibly highly paid due to the large number of times they will be seen by customers and the huge budgets involved. Television commercials may be extremely hard to book as a model, as they require confidence being filmed, with models often competing against professionally trained actors!

In my experience, commercials often start at £1000 but can go up to potentially anything at all – the highest-paid one I have seen was £60,000! A company may 'buy' the commercial to use in a different way once it has been produced, so it is important for models to stay on top of this.

Videos

With the rise of social media and the internet, online videos have largely taken over TVCs. Models are booked to film videos where they are presenting something, wearing clothes or acting, to be featured online. Models are also often booked to appear in music videos, where they may have to dance. Models may also feature in films, ranging from fashion films to being extras on movies.

Generally, models are paid more for video work than photographs as their 'image' is used in a different way and they can be bought again by the client later on.

Hair work

A lot of modelling jobs involve hair work, which can be anything from in-store presentations to huge international campaigns. Models will often have their hair styled, cut or coloured, which can result in damaged hair. It is very important for a model to always be fully aware of what the hairdresser plans on doing to their hair, with full agency knowledge.

Niche sectors

Once niche sectors of the modelling industry have recently grown in size, allowing for a more diverse range of models to be used. This is largely owing to social media and online modelling work, where customers want to see themselves represented in the fashion industry more than ever. These may include the following.

- Swim/lingerie
- Petite (5'8" and below)
- Curve/plus-sized (usually starting at a size 12. Some agencies may have specific boards for curve models, both men and women)
- Fitness
- Beauty (with work based on a model's face instead of their body)
- Hands/feet
- Promotions (involving being a waitress/hostess at events)
- Classical (targeting an older audience, often above the age of 30 but potentially any age)
- Bridal
- Maternity (often using a fake 'bump' – models do not have to be pregnant)
- Influencer (see 'I is for Instagram').

Anti-exploitation tips

- Think of modelling as a long-term career – identify what your ultimate goals are and how you can get there. Be realistic about your chances of success; for example, if you are under 5'7" it may be a waste of time attempting to become a catwalk model.

- Consider what you want from modelling and actively choose that career. For me, I just wanted to make money on the side of my other commitments and do professional work with no pressure, so I found a small, commercial agency. Do your research into which agencies work best in certain areas.

- Meet your agency once every few months to discuss your career strategy and what you want from your work.

- Ask to see your booking agreement (see 'L is for Legal') to find out everything you can about the job.

- Research every job before attending, and set a realistic expectation. Ask your agency what to expect from a particular client if you are unsure and do not be afraid to tell the client it is your first time.

- Say no to anything you do not feel comfortable with, regardless of whether your agency has agreed this for you. Inform the client politely that you do not feel comfortable and do not allow them to pressure you.

- If you do not want to do a certain type of job, tell your agency! Likewise, if you do want to do a certain type of job more so than others. They are there to get you work.

- Understand what is a reasonable level of respect. If you feel uncomfortable, call your agency and never be afraid to walk out of a job.

- Understand what is reasonable work. If you are unable to go to the bathroom because you have so many pieces to shoot, this is not acceptable. Ensure that you always have an hour lunch break and take any breaks that you need, within reason.

- Stay off your phone while at work as you are being paid for your time and this will prevent you from being booked in the future.

- Study the poses of any new client on their website and social media channels to understand what they want from a model.
- Never let anyone change the way you look without your agency knowing.
- Undertake courses in confidence or acting if you are feeling nervous – doing an acting course helped prepare me for television commercial work.
- Speak to other models about their experiences and learn from them.

is for Knowing What to Expect

I FIGURED OUT what to expect from modelling after years of trial and error. No one ever sits down and explains to you what to expect while working, what is acceptable and what is not. It took me years of tentatively turning up to castings, sending pleading emails after weeks of no contact or months of not being paid, being told to strip down in front of strangers and being poked, prodded and pushed on a daily basis by different people in the course of my job to understand when I can and should speak out.

In this chapter, I will explain what to expect as professional conduct in the course of a modelling career, in order for models to protect themselves against exploitative and potentially dangerous situations that they may not have otherwise been able to identify as wrong.

Did you know?

1. Many models are completely unprepared when starting out and have no idea what to expect, working it out as they go along.

2. Models find out their schedules the evening before, every day.

3. It is very rare for models to see booking agreements with the full details of a job, which makes it difficult for them to know what to expect, as well as for the client, who is sent an unprepared model.

4. Models are often sent last-minute castings and jobs with less than one hour's notice.

5. Models are rarely given feedback from their agency or clients.

What to expect after joining an agency

Once a model is signed to an agency, they will be placed on a specific 'board', for example, Development, New Faces or Mainboard. These relate to the amount of experience a model has, how much they will work and what kind of rates they will receive. Different bookers manage different boards, usually with a division between men and women models.

The model will be introduced to their relevant booker(s) who will be their main point of contact. Their booker(s) should confirm all of their measurements and personal details, have fresh 'digital' pictures taken, ensure their contract is signed and start working for the model! If a model has changed from another agency their bookers may request all of their previous high-resolution images to be sent over and create them a portfolio with composite cards to take to castings. The agency will also upload the model's images to their website, where each model has their own profile page in order for clients to view their portfolio and measurements online.

They will propose the model for work when they are free, usually booking them on test shoots and castings initially, especially if the model is brand-new. There may be a long period where the model doesn't work at all – potentially months – as they build up their portfolio. Bookers should contact their models regularly, especially if they have no other commitments, such as university. I would say it is normal to go for three days without hearing from your bookers at all if you are free to work – although I once went for three weeks without hearing anything!

Models usually receive a daily schedule email from their agencies around 5–6pm if they have anything on the next day. This can be very frustrating and anxiety-inducing as models wait for an email that may not arrive, unable to make any plans of their own until this time! If a model wants to do something outside of modelling – anything from lunches to holidays – they will have to 'book out' this time by telling their agency in advance. Otherwise, bookers assume models are free at any time, on any day of the week and expect them to be available for last-minute work.

The daily schedule email will detail any appointments, castings, test shoots or jobs the model will have the next day. Usually very limited information is given, such as the name of the client and the address. Models will have to reply to confirm they have received the email. They can and should check their schedules by asking their bookers what 'is on their chart' for the week ahead.

Their bookers should be able to tell them what 'options' they are currently holding, as jobs often are not confirmed until a few days beforehand. Options mean that they have been shortlisted for a job and it is normally very hard for a model to cancel, even though they have a roughly 50% chance of being booked.

The above services are always free – a model should never, ever pay their agency any money.

What to have in your bag

As work is so last-minute, it is important for models to always be prepared for castings and jobs. They can do this by having the following in their bag at all times.

- Portfolio and composite cards. It may be worth investing in a tablet to carry this around easily.
- Natural make-up.
- Skin-toned underwear. For every single job, female models are required to wear skin-toned, seamless thongs.
- Nipple covers or a skin-toned or strapless bra. This is very helpful to ensure nipples are not seen. Usually models are expected not to wear a bra on jobs due to seeing it through the clothes.
- Phone chargers. Ideally both a portable and wall charger.
- Water and snacks.
- A book.
- Feminine hygiene products.
- If it is a winter season, 'hot packs', which are microwavable packages that can warm models up on cold jobs. You could even take along your own dressing gown and slippers, as sometimes the ones on set can be very unhygienic.

What to expect from a casting

Castings can literally involve anything at all. My very first casting required me to stand in front of ten strangers and tell them a joke. I've had to pretend to be in an enchanted forest, act as a spy, tell stories about my childhood, learn scripts, sing and do a cartwheel. This can be helpful in terms of building self-confidence; however, it can be dangerous if a model is expected to say yes to anything in the hope of booking work. I have experienced several humiliating, demeaning castings and it is important for models to be comfortable with saying no.

Usually, a casting will involve the model showing the client their portfolio and giving them a composite card. They may have to wait for a very long time, potentially hours, and usually are seen for roughly five minutes. They can be located anywhere from studios to private houses, and commonly involve a model trying on clothes and having their photograph taken.

Models will usually only be told the address and name of the client. Sometimes they may be told what the job is (such as a e-commerce photoshoot) and the dates it will take place. Very rarely will they be informed how much the job is paying before actually booking the job.

Models should recognise a potentially exploitative casting where someone is abusing their position of power. They should never have to attend castings they do not feel comfortable with (I always advise saying no to castings in private locations such as hotel rooms) and never have to undress in front of anyone or do anything at all that makes them feel uncomfortable, such as kissing a stranger. By researching the client and location beforehand, models can ensure they are legitimate.

Most castings result in rejection, with models having to attend around 15 to book a single job. Clients do not give feedback to the model and models often have several castings in one day to attend, all over a city. Female models are usually expected to wear heels at castings and all models are expected to look their best.

What to expect from a job

As a model, you will usually find out about jobs from your daily schedule. You may receive a 'call sheet', detailing the people and locations involved in the job, or the 'mood board', which shows the style that the client is aiming to achieve from the job. However, in my experience, most models are just told the location, client, call time and payment rate. Some agencies will not inform their models of the payment rate, so they have to reply to the email and ask. Extremely good agencies will send over a 'booking confirmation' for the model to sign, which details all of the terms of the job; however, most will sign this on behalf of the model. I never even knew that booking agreements existed until I started writing this book and it would have helped enormously for me to know what my rights and responsibilities were on jobs over the past 13 years. You can find a sample booking confirmation agreement in 'L is for Legal'.

The agency should confirm in advance with you anything unusual about the job, such as if it involves lingerie or shooting in a foreign country, but they don't always do this. I have turned up to jobs and have been driven hours out of the city, pressured to kiss other models and to wear see-through clothes with no prior notice!

Models should ask their agents for the booking agreement, call sheet, mood board and booking form for each job in order to fully prepare themselves for a job. They can also research the client online to learn about their brand and figure out their transport for the next day, aiming to be 15 minutes early.

They are expected to turn up to the job fully prepared with dry hair and clean skin, so it is always advisable to have a shower the night before, removing any nail varnish. Proper food and a good night's sleep are essential for a model's performance.

What to expect on a photoshoot

Models will turn up to a shoot at their 'call time' to find a team of people they probably haven't met before waiting for them. The client should always introduce themselves and the team to the model, giving them an introduction to the day ahead. Shoots are either in a studio or 'on location', which can be anywhere – from a bowling alley to a street alley.

The model will start in hair and make-up, possibly having people working on their hair, face and nails at the same time. Models do not have a say in how they look, as these professionals are following instructions from the client; however, they should have the opportunity to speak out about any allergies or issues they may have with the professionals' work, such as checking if make-up brushes have been washed (see 'Q is for Questions').

When they are ready, they will get changed into their first outfit. Models should be provided with a private changing room; however, this is often not the case. Females are expected to always wear skin-coloured thongs and no bras on shoots, with males usually expected to wear white boxers. They should always feel comfortable to request a proper changing area, no matter what.

Sometimes a dresser or stylist will help the model get changed, who the model should feel comfortable with asking for privacy. Stylists often have a serious degree of personal contact with a model, potentially touching all over a model's body – anything from fixing underwear seams to rubbing a lint roller over their chest. This should always be done with permission of the model and professionalism, if legitimately required.

The model will start shooting, where the photographer may instruct them on how to pose, showing them where to stand on set (usually marked by tape). It is helpful for models to see the 'mood boards' and gain an understanding of what the client wants. They are very rarely ever shown the photographs taken of them during or immediately after a job, unless they appear on a computer automatically. The model will never get to choose which images they want to be used!

Once they have the shot, the model will get changed into their next outfit. Shooting days may involve anywhere from a few to 100 outfit changes, so it is important that the model changes quickly. They almost never get to choose their outfits and it is expected that models love the clothes they are wearing! Models should always feel comfortable to say if certain clothes make them feel uncomfortable to wear, such as being see-through. The stylist, make-up artist and hair stylist will continue 'touching up' the model throughout the shoot to ensure they are looking their best. Clothes may be pinned into place as they don't always fit and models are very often expected to wear shoes that are too small or too big for them.

Breaks and lunch should be provided for the model, when they can rest. This is usually different on each job, with some clients providing full catering and others providing a lunch voucher.

Models will often be spoken about on shoots by many people as though they are not there, as everyone is looking for something different in the model. They essentially are acting as a commercial object for the day, and nothing should be taken personally. However, it is important to recognise abusive behaviour – I once had a client spend hours telling me off for having uneven eyebrows! Anything that causes a model serious upset should be made clear to the client, as they do not have permission to abuse a model just because they have booked them.

Shoots should be fun for models, having their photo taken in beautiful clothes. However, they should always be able to speak out and be heard by everyone on a shoot and respected as a human being rather than a product. Most professional UK-based clients are very good at providing models with appropriate care on shoots.

After a photoshoot you will wait for a certain period of time for the images to be published, which you can ask the client about on the day. The client may send the images to your agency who will use them for your portfolio, however it is important to always ask your agency to send you high-resolution images of the work you have done, as they won't automatically send these over to you. You will need these images if you choose to change agency in the future.

What to expect at a show

There will usually be at least around five models in any one show, and they will receive an introduction from the client upon arrival, several hours before the show begins. The models will go into hair and make-up backstage, usually with large teams of different make-up artists and hair stylists. During the rehearsal they will be taught the walking order, the music and the mood of the show. They will also have a fitting to try on all of the clothes and shoes that have been assigned to them. Models should always feel able to tell the client if they do not feel comfortable in any of the clothes and do not have to wear anything they don't want to.

There will usually be a running order of outfits and photos listed backstage showing the order that models will walk in. Models will all normally have a dresser who will help them change, which can be stressful as models may have seconds to change between walking. They should always have a private changing area, yet this is often not enforced – sometimes models even have their photograph taken as they change backstage, which is not okay. Female models are expected to wear a nude thong and no bra underneath clothes, with males in white boxers.

When the show begins, there will normally be a 'line-up' of models waiting to go on, where they will strut down the runway, pose at the end and return, before running like a headless chicken to get changed backstage!

Fashion shows typically last around 20 minutes and models generally have between two and ten outfits per show. See 'W is for Walk' for more on fashion shows.

Transparency

Ultimately, models will have a better understanding of their own job and therefore be less open to exploitation when the entire industry is more transparent. This can be done by models being treated as humans instead of products, having a full explanation about the industry and different areas of work and asked what they want from modelling. On a daily basis, if models viewed their own individual job contracts, and actually understood them, this would dramatically improve the state of transparency within the industry. We will discuss this in the next chapter.

Anti-exploitation tips

- Ask your agency to explain everything you need to know about the modelling industry and what your options are with regards to the strategy of your career. Ask them to inform you as soon as possible about any jobs you may have (instead of the day before) and to give you as much information as they can, ideally the booking agreement for each job.

- Inform your agency if you do not want to do anything at all, no matter how irrelevant it may seem, such as a fear of animals.
- Be prepared to work at the very last minute, booking off any personal appointments in advance.
- Always ask how the images are being used on a job, and if anything sounds out of the ordinary (e.g., a billboard when you thought it was for e-commerce), tell your agency immediately.
- Ensure that people ask your permission if they are touching you and speak up about anything at all that makes you feel uncomfortable.
- Remember everyone's name and treat them all with respect on a job, expecting the same in return. See 'Q is for Questions' for guidance on this.
- Be as professional as possible while at work. Put your phone on charge on the other side of the room, avoid wasting time and never chew gum on set, especially while being photographed.
- Treat the clothes with respect at all times, taking care with your make-up and hanging them on the coat hanger.
- Avoid bending, sitting down or putting your shoes on in new outfits as it will crease the clothes and they will have to be re-steamed.
- Remember that you are always entitled to a private changing room and regular breaks, including a lunch break.
- Remember that you can say no to anything, especially dangerous situations such as someone steaming clothes while you are wearing them.
- Always ask the team if you are able to post anything on social media from the shoot in advance of doing so, as often shoots are top-secret until they are published.

is for Legal

LEGALLY SPEAKING, MODELLING is a minefield. Models often sign over their power of attorney to their agency in their contracts, which means they do not usually see or even know about the contracts that involve them – such as foreign agency contracts or individual job bookings. The agency takes on no legal liability, which remains fully with the model – meaning that they can be liable for things they don't even know about!

There are no clear regulations on the UK modelling industry and because the job is on such a global scale, it is very difficult to understand what is a fair and legitimate contract or standard industry practice as opposed to exploitative and dangerous. Models tend to join agencies at a very young age[31] and do not properly understand their contracts – and neither do their parents.

---

[31] The Model Alliance, '2012 Industry Survey, Industry Analysis'. http:// modelalliance.org/industry-analysis; 56% of 241 surveyed models began working age 16 or below.

The industry is extremely specialised and may require expensive, specialist lawyers to explain the real implications of confusing modelling contracts.

In this chapter, I will explain how to understand complicated contracts, how greater transparency can be achieved for models to empower and protect them and how to avoid exploitation. If you do not know the legal terms of your work, you cannot ever fully understand it and are open to limitless exploitation. You can find and print out samples of contracts on www.themodelmanifesto.com to take to your agency yourself.

Did you know?

1. With the model's power of attorney, their agency can enter them into legal contracts without even telling them.

2. Models may be fully legally liable for all issues that may arise at work, for example, if they refuse to do a job they do not want to do.

3. Model agencies operate under employment agency law,[32] but there are currently no other clearly applicable regulations to the modelling industry specifically, despite the young age of many models.

4. The UK actors' and models' union, Equity,[33] can help member models with contractual and legal issues, including reading over contracts free of charge. See 'U is for Unionising' for more.

5. Models rarely see any contracts involving them after signing their mother agency contract, which they often do not understand or take seriously, and which can be very long and unfair.

---

[32] The Employment Agencies Act 1974. www.legislation.gov.uk/ukpga/1973/35
[33] Equity Models Network. www.equity.org.uk/getting-involved/networks/models-network/

How to understand a mother agency contract

A mother agency retains the final say on decisions regarding a model regardless of which other agencies a model is signed to. A contract is required to be in place with a mother agency's models in order to act on their behalf and define their relationship, otherwise it has no legal basis to act.

Unfortunately, due to the excitement of becoming a model and finding an agency, many models do not read the contract properly and as a result may freely sign themselves up to exploitation. The contracts may be unfairly biased, very confusing to understand and can even include terms such as having to maintain particular measurements in order to be paid. Ultimately, the contract is how to tell if an agency is operating legitimately. UK mother agency contracts may include terms such as the following:

Relationship between the model and the agent

- The model appoints the agency as their exclusive *personal manager*.
- The model is *self-employed*.
- The model allocates the agency their *power of attorney*, which means the agency can enter the model into contracts on the model's behalf.
- The model may or may not be allowed to work with other agencies/clients outside of the agency. Many contracts are *exclusive*, which means the model should refer all offers of work to the agency.
- The relationship is one of independent contractors.

The obligations of the model

- Obligations may include maintaining appearance in accordance with agency advice, being available for work at all times unless booked out or sick with a doctor's certificate and abiding with general professionalism at all times. If a model does not fulfil these, this may potentially result in termination of the contract.

- The contract may include terms on how the agency can be spoken about by the model. If they can never legally say anything derogatory (negative) about the agency, this is a cause for concern!
- The model is *fully legally responsible* for themself and their own expenses, including entering into the contract, registering as self-employed, paying tax and working visas. UK agencies do not withhold any money for National Insurance or tax (see 'T is for Tax').
- The model allows the agency to *handle the model's finances*, including collecting money from clients, deducting expenses from payments and holding money in the agency bank account for the model.
- The model understands that the agency does *not guarantee payment* from clients and is not responsible if a client doesn't pay.
- The model gives the agency the permission (a *licence*) to use the model's image (sometimes referred to as likeness) for agreed purposes such as promoting them, and to sell this licence to clients.
- The model gives permission for the agency to use the model's *personal data* in accordance with the relevant laws.

The obligations of the agency

- The agency promises to do its best to find the model work but has *no obligation* of doing so.
- The agency will give the model *advice* regarding the model's career.
- The agency can *sign contracts* relating to work, *invoice clients*, *sue clients* and *receive payment* on the model's behalf.
- The agency will *cover its own running costs* but any extra costs that are paid to a third party (such as an external photographer) can be paid for a model by the agency. See 'E is for Expenses'.

- The agency can sign the model to *another model agency* on the model's behalf, in a different country if they wish to do so.

The payment process

- Defining how models are paid – usually by bank transfer on a weekly/monthly basis. See 'F is for Finance'.
- Defining the maximum amount of time a model may have to wait to be paid after doing a job; for many agencies this is *90 days*. Once the agency has been paid by the client, it must pay the model within ten working days, by law – but it is hard to prove if the agency has been paid by the client and some contracts exclude this regulation.
- Defining the *commission rate* and how this is calculated, in addition to any other fees.
- Defining what happens in case of *non-payment* when the agency has to take a client to court on behalf a model – who usually pays the legal fees!

Termination of the contract

- May include an *initial/minimum term* that cannot be broken until it is finished, which is very important to question as the model will be bound for that period. Usually UK model contracts are on a rolling basis until termination by either side.
- Defining how the contract can be *terminated*, usually by written notice and a notice period.
- Defining for what reasons the contract can be *immediately terminated*. Usually the model agency can end a contract if the model is not fulfilling their obligations. A good contract will allow a model to terminate if the agency is not fulfilling its obligations.
- Defining the various obligations that will *continue* after termination, such as the requirement for the agency to pay the model any money owed. The model will normally have to fulfil their options for work with their agency.

Liability

- Defining *legal liability* (responsibility) in case either party encounters a legal issue. Agencies tend to limit their liability for everything they can within the law, such as loss of business, profit, revenues, failure by a client or a model to attend a booking and non-payment. Models often tend to be fully legally liable in all circumstances!

Confidentiality

- Defining what is *confidential information* and must be kept between the parties; usually includes confidential business information of the agency and any of its clients.

General

- List of terms that are defined, such as *territory*.
- Terms relating to *force majeure* – something unforeseeable happening that breaches the contract with no fault on either side.
- Terms relating to *sever-ability*, where if parts of the contract are not upheld in court the rest of it will be ineffective.
- The *geographical jurisdiction* and *law* that the contract falls under.

Signature

- A contract needs signatures from both parties in order to become *binding*. If a model is under 18 their parent may need to sign on their behalf and there may also be a witness signature required.

How to understand agency terms and conditions

An agency's terms and conditions can normally be found on its website. These generally cover all jobs that the agency books and may discuss the following.

- Booking fees: how fees work with regards to a daily/hourly rate and what this involves – usually an eight-hour period between 9am and 6pm. They may also refer to overtime and weekend/bank holiday rates.
- Location bookings: how a model will travel for work, such as the client providing transport and undertaking a proper health and safety assessment of the location. Visas will also be discussed, which is very important in case of models working abroad.
- Additional fees: any additional fees for a job, such as in different territories and social media postings.
- Agency fees: how the agency commission is calculated.
- Invoices: how an agency invoices a client and the terms of payment, such as the payment period.
- Provisional bookings: refers to options and how the booking process works.
- Cancellations: what happens if a model/client cancels. Often cancellations fees apply if a confirmed job is cancelled.
- Meals: whether models are fed on jobs.
- Model care and safety: discussing the general welfare of a model, including nudity and reputation.
- Fashion shows, films and music videos: the rights and usage rates of models in these types of work.
- Test photography: how photographers are allowed to use images from test shoots – generally not for any commercial purposes.
- Intellectual property rights: usage rights.
- Insurance and liability: relating to insurance on jobs. The client will generally be required to have insurance and may be liable for any injury caused to a model on a job. Agencies often absolve themselves of all liability to the client.

Understanding a secondary agency agreement

Modelling involves travelling around the world, working for different clients. Mother agencies can contract models out to other agencies in different markets to find them work, which can be complicated for both the agent and model to understand in terms of the specific obligations, international law and problems that may occur.

A typical secondary model agency agreement will include the provisions of a mother agency agreement in addition to a term stating that the model/mother agency appoint the secondary agency to act as the model's exclusive manager for that specific territory. The two agencies agree that commission rate will be automatically paid to the mother agency by the secondary agency for all jobs undertaken by the model. The responsibility for the model to secure a valid working visa is the model's own, as seen in 'V is for Visas'.

As seen in 'O is for Overseas', some models may have contracts for set fees with the secondary agency. This is usually a guarantee that they will earn a certain amount of money overall by going 'on stay' with that agency for a particular period of time through jobs booked by the agency. Sometimes these contracts are not fulfilled and the agency will supplement the payment but as the guarantee does not usually include agency expenses, this doesn't often happen.

These types of contracts, although sounding tempting, are very dangerous because if the model does not make this money, for any reason, they may have to pay it – and the contracts are usually very complicated and unfair to the model. Foreign agencies operate under different human rights laws and can include incredibly unfair terms such as a model having to maintain unrealistic measurements in order to be paid. Models will have to do all of the work booked for them under the contracts, which may involve three jobs per day or escort-type jobs.

There are also often lots of expenses that are deducted by the agency, so generally models do not make as much money as they expect. Due to the international nature of the contract it is very difficult to enforce and to secure payment once a model has left the country.

Models do not often see these contracts, so it is critically important that if your agency wishes to send you 'on stay' to a new country, you ask to sign the contract yourself before going.

Understanding a non-disclosure/ confidentiality agreement

Models may be given these types of agreements on jobs of a confidential nature, such as involving celebrities or unreleased designer collections. They usually include the names and addresses of each party and contain an obligation not to disclose any information at all to anyone at all for a certain period of time, usually forever.

It is very important that these are read and understood fully before signing, because you could be sued for the smallest of things even if they seem innocent, such as posting any picture at all from the shoot online. The model cannot post or disclose anything to anyone about the job once they have signed such an agreement and can be sued for a lot of money if they break it. It is advisable to only sign a non-disclosure agreement if you feel 100% comfortable that you can and will adhere to it, which means not signing if someone has done something that makes you feel uncomfortable that you may like to report in the future.

Any agreements given to you on a job should be checked with your agency before you sign anything.

How to understand your legal relationship with a client

Most models are completely unaware that they have a legal relationship with their clients, as they do not know there is a contract in place – even if it is implied (not written down). An agency owes its models a duty of care, which is a legal and moral obligation to ensure their wellbeing and safety, which extends to vetting clients. As the model is self-employed, they are independent during the course of their work and so once they are on a job, the client owes them the duty of care to ensure they are being looked after.

This stems from employment law and the contract that is signed by the agency, and can become extremely complicated if there is no booking agreement in place to refer back to.

For every job a model does, an individual contract is negotiated and agreed by the agency, including the details of the job – the rate of pay and time of the booking. This can come in various forms: a booking agreement, a model release form or an informal email agreement covered under the agency terms and conditions – there is no general standard and every job and agency is different. This can become very complicated if a problem arises.

A booking agreement (also sometimes referred to as a job contract, model release form or usage agreement) details the exact nature and details of the job. These forms explain what has been negotiated and involve vital details such as names, addresses and promises from each party. It is very helpful for models to see these forms; however, they often receive nothing but the minimum details.

Each agreement details what the usage is for a job – how the work can be used and for how long. If a client wants to extend the usage for a job, they must pay more money to the agency and model, so it is important for a model to be aware of potential income. For example, I once was surprised to see my images on a billboard in central London that had been taken for a look-book – I had no idea that the client should have paid more for this! Models generally have no idea what the agreed usage is for the jobs that they do.

Usage requires an extremely honest and transparent relationship between the model, agency and client – agents often do not want to antagonise clients and cut themselves off to future work so a lot of usage breaches are permitted, to the model's detriment. It is also very hard to keep on top of how work is being used by a client, especially if it is in a different country.

The clients must be trusted to inform the agents of any extra usages in addition to keeping on top of their own usage practices, for example, taking down images on their website after one year has passed. If they are booking models every day, it is hard to keep track of this! Furthermore, the agency must be trusted to pass on these extra payments to the model, who may no idea that they have been paid, especially if they have left the agency. If models know of the agreed usage, they can help their agency keep track.

Booking agreement for modelling services

A typical booking agreement may include the below sections. I advise taking the sample template on www.themodelmanifesto. com to your agency and asking them to send you a booking agreement for every job, as it details:

- How much the client is paying to hire you, *in total*, including the agency fee (which is rarely disclosed to models).
- *All* details of a job, including the team involved and anything unusual, such as nudity and how the images will be used (which is how the fee has been agreed). If the client uses images in a way that has not been agreed, they should pay more money to the agency and model as a 'buyout'.

A legitimate agency that trusts its models should have no issue with them knowing this information as they are working to protect you and ensure that you are paid the money that you are owed.

Introduction

This booking is offered subject to the Agency's terms and conditions and is required to be signed by the client at least 12 hours prior to the start of any job.

Details

- Model/Agency:
- Client:
- Date of booking:
- Time of booking start/finish:
- Location:
- Team:
- Summary of booking (including anything unusual, such as the number of looks/images and what kind of job it is, such as e-commerce, and anything for the model to note, such as the need to bring particular shoes or underwear to the job):

Usage

- Usage agreement (how the work can be used by the client, for example, online or just on social media. Includes how long the image can be used for, in which geographic area and any competitors that the model is not allowed to work for as a result):
- Usage rate (the amount of money a client pays to use the images in the above way):
- Buy-out fee (the amount of money a client will pay if they wish to buy the images to use in a different way; sometimes this is agreed later):

Payment

- Day rate (amount the model is paid per day of work):

- Usage rate (as above):
- Expenses (things covered by the client for the model, for example, train tickets to the job, the receipts for which will need to be sent to the client with the invoice):
- Total amount chargeable to client (this will include the above and the agency fee. The model will normally receive around 65% of this figure).

By having a booking confirmation in place, models, clients and agencies are protected. In the world of social media and exposés, it is more important than ever for legitimate clients to protect themselves against models who are unaware of what has been agreed with the client. Models can understand their own contracts and have a say in their own careers, and agencies can protect themselves against accusations of mismanagement. As we will see in the next chapter, often there is miscommunication between the agency and model that can result in terrible consequences.

Anti-exploitation tips

- Read every contract that you receive – and if you don't receive one, ask for it! If there is something you don't understand or that appears alarming, try to discuss the contract with a friend who has some legal experience or the free legal advisors at Equity before you speak to the agency.
- Understand that you can negotiate your contract – the agency would not be signing you if it did not really want to represent you.
- If you have queries about your contract that you feel you should raise with the agency, ask them to explain it to you. If they say it 'doesn't apply to you', then ask them to cross out that section before signing.
- Remember that you are self-employed and ultimately legally responsible for yourself, particularly regarding your conduct

while at work. If you breach one of these contracts you can be sued personally by the client or the agency.

- Ask for every legally binding document that involves you and file them all electronically. Understand the usage that has been agreed for every job and keep track of it by following the client on social media and checking in with their websites once the date has passed. Create a spreadsheet of the links to your work and the dates that the usage expires, with alerts in your calendar to remind you of this.
- Refer any legal issues to Equity, who provide free legal assistance to model members. See 'U is for Unionising'.
- Keep on track with your agency account and any expenses that are charged in your name. Ask your agency to send you a statement of this account every month and ask them to not charge any expenses without informing you first and definitely not over a maximum amount. Be very careful when modelling abroad – nothing is for free! See 'E is for Expenses'.
- Read the terms and conditions on your agency website to understand whether they sound legitimate or not.
- If you are ever given an agreement to sign while on a job always be sure to check it with your agency first before signing.
- Never risk breaching a non-disclosure agreement, even if you feel that it is not breaking it exactly. Take all legal agreements very seriously.
- Just because an agency may have a good reputation, be nice people or appear to be a legitimate business does not mean that the contract won't exploit you. Take all of your contracts very seriously and remember that they are legally binding. I have been told many times by agencies that they are just a 'formality' and 'don't mean anything', but they definitely do and can result in extremely bad situations.
- Ask your agency to send you a booking agreement for every job that you do.
- Check on jobs how the images will be used by asking the client.

is for Measurements

PROTRUDING BONES, GAPING thighs and skeletal faces are what people normally associate with the exploitation of models.

Ironically, models are rarely ever weighed. Their weight is not an issue in terms of numbers on a scale, yet it is constantly hanging over them in the form of measurements – the magic numbers on a tape slid around their body.

Measurements are a very unreliable way of weighing up someone's ability to work, especially because everyone measures differently and our measurements fluctuate every day. Holding the measuring tape at a slightly different point on the hips can lead to a centimetre being added, with models being told that they cannot work unless they 'fix' their measurements. Every model that I know has had struggles with fitting the unrealistic measurements required of them.

In this chapter, I will explain what it means to be told to 'tone up', how to deal with weight pressure and how to protect yourself from those wishing to use this to exploit you.

Did you know?

1. Models are regularly told to 'fix their measurements' or 'tone up' by their agencies.[34]

2. Female fashion models are generally expected to be between a size six and eight, unless they are 'plus-sized', which starts at a size twelve. They are required to be above 5'8" in height (ideally 5'11").

3. There are no clear requirements for male models other than to be over 5'11" in height.

4. Clients and agencies may require a model to lose weight.

5. Models may be prevented from working until they have the right measurements, meaning they are not promoted to clients and are unable to attend castings.

6. Models may be referred to personal trainers and nutritionists in order to reach certain measurements, potentially paying very high fees.

What are the ideal measurements?

Models are essentially like athletes – their body is their work. They are booked for jobs primarily based on how they look in clothes, which means that they have to meet the demands of their clients. This is complicated by the fact that models are human beings as well as products, and often vulnerable ones at that – they have

---

[34] Rachel F. Rodgers, Sara Ziff, Alice S. Lowy, Kimberly Yu and S. Bryn Austin, 'Results of a strategic science study to inform policies targeting extreme thinness standards in the fashion industry', *International Journal of Eating Disorders*, Vol. 50, No. 3 (2017): 284–292.

a variety of people trying to profit from the way they look and moulding this to their wants.

Every agency is different in what it will and will not accept from its models in terms of measurements, but below are the traditionally 'standard' requirements.

Standard female fashion model measurements are a 34" bust, 24" waist and 34" hips, and a height of over 5'8". Models with these measurements will likely have a very low BMI[35] and it is incredibly hard to maintain these unnatural measurements. Many models join agencies while they are still teenagers, and puberty means their body will change – which in turn affects their jobs.

Plus-sized modelling has become more popular as many top retailers have brought out 'curve' divisions, with some top agencies even having dedicated 'curve' boards. Female models generally should be at least a size 12 to be on this board, whereas there is no clearly defined requirement for males. Curve models are often told to put on weight.

Female measurements are taken by measuring the chest (over the nipples), the smallest part of the waist and the biggest part of the hips (the bum – not the bones slightly higher up). Height is measured by a measuring device attached to the wall. One problem that models encounter is that there is no consistency in how they are measured – one booker may measure them loosely whereas another may measure them slightly higher up on their body. The centimetre difference can mean they aren't sent out to castings and are encouraged to lose weight.

Male models have a much more difficult time in general understanding what is required of them in terms of measurements – they should be over 5'10" tall (and ideally as tall as possible), but everything else is questionable. Their chest, waist, suit and inside-leg measurements are noted but are not as important as for

[35] NHS, 'What is the body mass index (BMI)?' www.nhs.uk/common-health-questions/lifestyle/what-is-the-body-mass-index-bmi/

female models, because men's sizes vary dramatically depending on their kind of work. They tend to either be required to be very thin or very muscular.

Male models are measured around the widest part of their chest and smallest part of their waist. Agencies often have unreliable measurements for models listed on their profiles on the agency website, which is part of why castings are so important.

Models regularly have their measurements taken by their agency and clients. As long as they are working, there should never be an issue. High-fashion, editorial and catwalk clients tend to be stricter on measurements than more commercial, catalogue-type clients. Though it is good to maintain a healthy diet and regular exercise, if a model is asked to change their weight it should involve serious consideration. It is very difficult to lose weight, especially if someone is already slim, and many models develop serious eating disorders as a result.

Why do models have to fit certain measurements?

Models are ultimately a product for an agency and clients, who expect them to take their job seriously. When there is a 'problem', such as measurements that are too big for clients, the agency has to relay this to the model. Essentially, it all comes down to business.

Some models may be instructed to put on weight, especially if they are plus-sized – which can be just as dangerous! As plus-sized female models start at size 12, they are often too small to accurately represent this industry and have to wear padding on set. Some male models in particular are often instructed to gain muscle, which could lead to dangerous practices such as taking steroids. For the purposes of this book, I will discuss losing weight, but the same advice applies to putting on weight.

There are several reasons a model may be instructed to lose weight. I was told to lose three inches off my hips (which were 37") by one agency after they'd scouted me, as their requirement for taking me on. This took me over six months to do, and I was measured every week in front of the agency to no avail. I was sent to a personal trainer and desperately tried to lose the weight, which came straight back on once I had reached the desired measurements through starving myself. I didn't understand why I had to be this size, nor how to maintain it.

Other agencies did not ask me to lose weight in this way – only when a very important client requested it and gave me a couple of months to do so. Frustratingly, the client didn't give any requirements other than to 'tone up', so my agency would send them images of me in a bikini every few weeks until they were happy. This was a much easier process as I really wanted to work for the client and understood the reasoning behind it, despite having serious body dysmorphia as a result.

There is no standardisation of measurement practices across the industry. Some agencies regularly measure models and will prevent them from working if they are not the right measurements, as they believe that this will ruin the impression of both the model and the agency for potential clients. One agency may require a model to be certain measurements where another may not; I began working immediately when I changed model agency, despite my measurements previously having prevented me from working for six months. Generally, high-fashion modelling requires much stricter measurements than commercial modelling, as seen in 'J is for Jobs'.

A model can be told to lose weight at any time, for any reason. Potential reasons include:

- An agency requiring certain measurements to represent models.
- Models not booking work.

- Clients requesting it or an agency receiving negative feedback from clients.
- A model travelling to a new market with different measurement requirements.
- A change in a model's measurements.

There is a very tricky line between models maintaining their fitness in order to work well and being controlled by their measurements. If they do not need to lose weight in order to work at their desired level, they should not have work withheld from them; however, they rely on the expertise of their agency to strategise their career for them. It ultimately boils down to the relationship a model has with their agency, as seen in 'A is for Agency'.

How are models told to lose weight?

There is no right way to tell someone to lose weight. The biggest issue regarding measurements is often miscommunication, with models not understanding what is required of them or why.

The most common way models are instructed lose weight is by being told to 'tone up', as 69.4% of surveyed models had been,[36] which some take literally – often resulting in increased measurements as models build muscle from exercise.

It is crazy to assume that models would be able to drop a specific amount of inches off their body in particular areas only without the use of a liposuction procedure. Models are often given time periods, such as a few weeks, to reach their target measurements and are taken off the casting circuit to be able to 'focus'. Some

---

[36] Rachel F. Rodgers, Sara Ziff, Alice S. Lowy, Kimberly Yu and S. Bryn Austin, 'Results of a strategic science study to inform policies targeting extreme thinness standards in the fashion industry', *International Journal of Eating Disorders*, Vol. 50, No. 3 (2017): 284–292; 54.1% of surveyed models had been advised that they lose weight, 63.1% were told that they would be more successful if they lost weight, 21.2% were told their agency would stop representing them unless they lost weight, 7.2% had been given pills, dietary supplements or substances to help them lose weight by their agency.

may feel they are being punished and deprived of work, resulting in a cycle of crash diets, guilt and depression.

Dangerous advice is often given to models on how they can best achieve these unrealistic demands, as it is unlikely that agents will have any proper training in exercise, health or nutrition. Various guidance I have heard over the years includes, 'only eat grapes until 3pm', 'don't eat any carbohydrates', 'avoid bread' and 'just drink water'. Other myths include models being told to eat cotton wool as it expands in their stomachs, and living off an apple per day. A good agency will not instruct a model in this unprofessional way.

Models are often referred to different professionals by their agencies in order to reach the measurements healthily and sustainably. However, this can be problematic as these professionals tend to be very expensive, leaving models out of pocket and potentially accepting agency 'advances' for these services, which may come with interest rates, as seen in 'E is for Expenses'. Personal trainers and nutritionists may charge hundreds of pounds per hour. I have seen models being put on diets where food is delivered to their house at a cost of £30 per day!

The cycle continues as models are often prevented from working until their measurements are right, resulting in them having serious financial issues in addition to their weight. Models may also suffer significant mental heath issues due to this pressure, as seen in 'Z is for Zen'.

Additionally, these professionals may not be so professional. Modelling is a unique industry, requiring unique measurements, and it is hard to give advice to a model under severe pressure to lose inches from their body in a matter of weeks – there is not really a healthy way to do this. Many professionals that are referred to by model agencies may have a 'special relationship' with an agency, which can be beneficial if the model is receiving a discount but problematic if the professional is incited to draw out the process in order to receive more money or behave unprofessionally.

I have heard of agencies pressuring models to take drugs to lose weight, which is illegal. If an agency has a good relationship with professionals such as doctors, they may prescribe models drugs they do not need in order to lose weight. I have also witnessed models taking illegal drugs such as cocaine to control their weight, which is incredibly dangerous and unsustainable.

Many models end up in a cycle of starvation, with 56.5% of surveyed models skipping meals to lose weight.[37] I would starve myself until I was measured, then buy a box of chocolates on the way home! Starvation is very unhealthy and results in the entire body being affected – hair loss, skin problems, fatigue and even sudden death can result from not eating properly.

Eating disorders

Due to the pressure to fit certain measurements, many models develop eating disorders and body dysmorphia, feeling that they look a completely different way to how they look in reality. It is important to remember that both men and women suffer from these disorders.

I suffered with anorexia and bulimia throughout my teenage years, which I believe is largely because of the pressures I encountered from modelling. These illnesses have potentially lifelong side effects, including: downy hair on the face; dry, yellow skin; bloating; exhaustion; hair loss; disrupted menstrual cycles; and long-term fertility issues. Bulimics may also destroy their teeth,

---

[37] According to a study on eating disorders, 56.5% of surveyed models skipped meals within the last year to lose weight or change their body shape/size, 70.5% had dieted, 81.2% exercised, 51.7% went on fasts/cleanses/nutritional detoxes, 23.6% used weight loss supplements or diet pills, 16.6% used stimulants, 2.4% used intravenous drips, 8.2% made themselves throw up and 24.7% used other methods including laxatives and sweat suits. Rachel F. Rodgers, Sara Ziff, Alice S. Lowy, Kimberly Yu and S. Bryn Austin, 'Results of a strategic science study to inform policies targeting extreme thinness standards in the fashion industry', *International Journal of Eating Disorders*, Vol. 50, No. 3 (2017): 284–292.

throat and stomach due to the acid they activate when making themselves sick.

Anyone suffering with an eating disorder is at risk of death, and is putting their body through tremendous stress and suffering. It is so important that they receive help and support from those around them – whether a friend or a counsellor. I would recommend models to leave the industry for a while if they are suffering with an eating disorder, as the world of fashion is very unhealthy and triggering.

If you are suffering from an eating disorder, it is vitally important that you get help. Speak to your family, friends and doctor about how you feel. Your agency should never encourage you to be unwell and most legitimate agencies have support policies for models suffering with eating disorders, such as referrals to the charity BEAT,[38] which specialises in eating disorders. You should also seek the advice of your doctor and utilise the support available, such as counselling sessions.

How to maintain healthy measurements

The first thing you should ever do when faced with a suggestion to change your weight is to consider why this is being asked of you and if you want to do it.

If you trust your agency and agree with their suggestion that it would dramatically improve your career in the way that you want, consider whether this is something you would like to invest your energy into. A good agency should always offer you the option to cast with clients at the measurements you are, or will advise you to seek alternative representation if they don't believe you will work with their clients at your current measurements. They will treat you respectfully and communicate honestly with you, taking

---

[38] Beat Eating Disorders. https://www.beateatingdisorders.org.uk/

into consideration what you want from your own career and how realistic it is for you to change your body as suggested.

Consider all of your options – different agencies, different types of work or alternative careers altogether. Ensure you are being realistic and fully understand how hard it will be to reach certain measurements – it is likely to involve a lot of hard work and dedication for an indefinite amount of time in order to maintain these measurements.

If changing your measurements is something you still wish to do (regardless of anybody else), then engage in healthy eating and exercise. Make an attainable plan by researching online properly how you will do this, always prioritising your health. I would advise making it fun by taking up a form of exercise you enjoy, such as dancing.

Avoid dieting and especially skipping meals – make a healthy, sustainable lifestyle change if you wish to do so. The best way to do this is by education; by learning as much as I could about veganism, I changed the way I look at food and cured my sugar addiction. Be mindful about what you consume and how you feel afterwards.

It is also helpful to cook all of your own food (three meals per day!) and take this to castings/jobs with you, so that you are not tempted by unhealthy food. Research different meals online and cook in bulk on the weekends, so that you are prepared for the week ahead.

Carefully consider the benefits of using professionals such as nutritionists. I strongly believe that you can do this yourself with enough motivation and research. However, you should tell your support network, such as your family, about what you are doing, so they can ensure you stay healthy and reasonable.

As a model, you must take responsibility for your own career, body and health. By ensuring you are as healthy as possible, you will empower yourself to have a strong mind and body, making your own choices about your work and life. In the next chapter, I will demonstrate how you can make these choices in a wider context, improving your chances of employment inside and outside the modelling industry without being exploited.

Anti-exploitation tips

- If a model agency or client asks you to lose or gain weight, consider why. Think about whether the agency is doing its job properly, whether it has sent you on castings lately and whether your body may have changed lately and how you feel about this. Remember that people may try to blame you as a result of their own inadequacies.
- Make your own decisions about how you should look. If you feel happy and confident at certain measurements and are being asked to change, always feel empowered enough to say no. Do not let anyone pressure you into looking a certain way if you don't feel 100% comfortable and want to actually look that way. I personally hate having 34-inch hips as my bones stick out and I look and feel incredibly unwell.
- Do your research and choose your own career. If you want to take modelling as your full-time, serious career, understand that you will have to put in dedication and hard work for this. Alternatively, if you see modelling as a hobby, do not let anyone make it your life. Seek out agencies that will work for you.
- Never let anybody pressure you into spending money on a nutritionist, personal trainer or other professional in order to change how you look. Only see these people if you absolutely 100% want to, and always ask around for other options, as such professionals tend to be very expensive. If you do engage in these services, constantly assess their advice and whether it is worth continuing to pay for.
- If an agency says you cannot work at the measurements you are, leave. Another agency will most likely happily send you to work how you are! Different clients have different requirements and agencies can send you to all of them.

- Avoid alcohol, cigarettes and unprescribed drugs. If anyone offers you any in the course of your job, especially with regards to weight, always report this to your agency, Equity (see 'U is for Unionising') or the police.
- Avoid any unhealthy weight loss or gain methods, such as skipping meals or taking steroids. This is unsustainable and will seriously impact your health.
- Ensure that you have a strong support network, even if that is just one person. Tell them about any pressures you may be experiencing and ask them to check in regularly with you to ensure that you are healthy and are making the choices you want to make.
- Remember that almost every single model experiences pressures with regards to their weight, and you are not alone. Speak to your fellow models, especially those represented by your agency, to gain and provide support to one another.
- Remember that your self-worth consists of much more than numbers on a measuring tape. See 'Z is for Zen' for more advice on how to maintain a healthy mind.

is for Networking

MODELS HAVE UNPARALLELED access to celebrities, top designers and the elite of society. Over the course of a model's career they meet so many successful, talented and well-connected people that they have a unique opportunity to learn about different careers and get a foot into many doors.

However, models are also be likely to encounter exploitation by such powerful people, due to the vulnerable nature of their work. In this chapter, I will explain how to network professionally and recognise potentially dangerous situations.

Did you know?

1. Models often work with the owners and managers of extremely successful companies, fashion industry leaders and celebrities.

2. Models may be invited to, or work at, social events where alcohol or drugs are present.

3. Some models have no other qualifications or experience than modelling, due to starting at a young age and putting off further education.

What is networking and why is it important?

Networking involves interacting with others to exchange information and develop professional or social contacts. As models tend to be very young and inexperienced in their early years of work, it can be amazing for them to build contacts with highly successful people who can help them secure further job opportunities.

The modelling industry itself is often about who you know, which is partially why there is so much exploitation – certain individuals have the power to catapult your career, no experience necessary. More on this can be seen in 'S is for Sexual Exploitation'.

Models are under constant pressure to know what they will do after modelling, as it is commonly assumed that the job has a very short time span. While many models do leave the industry after a few years, many continue to have prosperous careers – I know very successful models in their thirties and personally find that I work much better the older I become. However, this looming pressure means that many models are very vulnerable as they personally identify with modelling and do not know a career outside of it. It is very different in the 'real world' and models may not be able to establish professional boundaries or recognise exploitative behaviour.

For those who do not wish to make modelling their main career in life, the potential that the job offers to work with and meet industry professionals is very valuable. As can be seen in 'Y is for Your Career', models work across a range of different industries and can gain experience from every opportunity for their CV. In just one day, a model may pitch themselves to a client in a casting, market themselves on social media, file their financial accounts and organise their flights and accommodation for an overseas trip. Through the variety within the job, models can understand which aspects they most enjoy and pursue these.

How can models network safely?

The best way to pursue careers of interest is by gaining professional work experience in the industry. Most jobs require prior experience in their general field and models work with a huge range of people on a daily basis – marketing managers, make-up artists, hairdressers, creative directors, agents, photographers and stylists, to name a few. They can capitalise on these encounters by using their connections to gain work experience in different areas and understand what they enjoy outside of modelling.

As models are self-employed, they can theoretically choose when they work. Combined with the rarity of paid jobs, many models enjoy a lot of free time and the opportunity to work a few days per month in order to support themselves financially, while booking out the rest of their time to work in other areas. This requires strong self-confidence, flexibility and dedication.

It is very hard to commit to other opportunities when your booker is pressuring you to work, or someone is offering you £1000 for one day in comparison to the minimum wage you may be making in an internship. By being confident enough to know you are investing in your future career, flexible enough to move around schedules if required and dedicated enough to your commitments, you can make educated decisions and gain experience in many areas at once. Most people in society do not enjoy the luxury of free time to figure out what they want to do, so it is very important to recognise the value of this and use it productively.

On a standard shoot, there will be a photographer, make-up artist, hair stylist, clothes stylist and possibly a designer or a creative director present. At fashion events, celebrities and industry leaders will often be present. These people, especially if they are highly successful, are likely to be very intimidating, so it is important to have a strong sense of confidence and professionalism. By being polite and speaking to the people on your jobs about their own careers, you can professionally enquire about the possibility of gaining work experience with someone.

Internships may lead to job opportunities and are very important for your CV. After I finished studying law, I used my connections to try out a variety of different careers to understand what they all involved. This bypassed online application procedures and enabled me to stand out from the crowd. I would advise always having an updated CV in your draft emails in case you come across an opportunity you like while on a job.

The best way to network professionally with someone at work is to ask if they would mind telling you a bit more about their career due to your interest in the area. Alternatively, you could outright ask someone for work experience; however, the best way to formalise this in a professional manner is to always obtain their email address and send a formal email following up your conversation, with your CV attached.

Below is a good example email.

> Dear (X),
>
> Thank you so much for taking the time to tell me about your career in (X) today during the (X) job. It was very inspiring to hear about your experiences and I would greatly appreciate the opportunity to learn more about the industry if you are able to offer a work experience placement or simply give any more advice.
>
> I greatly appreciate any assistance and look forward to hearing from you. I have attached my CV for your reference.
>
> Kindest wishes,
>
> (Y)

This formalises your relationship in writing and ensures there is a professional basis. Do not harass the person if they don't reply or can't offer you any more help and always inform your agency before contacting anyone from a photoshoot directly. People will generally be happy to help you out if they can, as they often remember how difficult it was when starting out – but it is very important that you are able to properly commit to any opportunities and to act professionally. If you don't network with the utmost professionalism and respect, you could jeopardise your career and reputation.

Networking is also a useful tool in terms of success as a model – people want to work with people they like, so it pays to befriend colleagues in order to solidify a regular client base. These connections can also refer a model for other jobs, so it is important for models to always be on top form, no matter how small the job may seem, as it could lead to much bigger things. These days, Instagram is the most common way to network, with teams following each other after jobs and tagging each other in the images. Although jobs can be intimidating, it is fairly easy to speak to people once you understand how; see 'Q is for Questions' for some great conversation starters.

To network specifically in terms of the modelling industry, it may be advisable to organise informal photoshoots or pass along opportunities that may be relevant to the people you meet at work. General professionalism on a job increases your chances of being rebooked, especially if you make an effort to stand out from other models, such as not going on your phone for the entire day or ensuring you hang up your clothes for the stylist. It is good to have a notebook with you on all jobs to write down the names and details of everyone you meet – especially the assistants, as they will be your future clients!

It is important to assess when networking can become dangerous. Many people may use these opportunities and positions of power to abuse models.

How can models be exploited through networking?

Models are often in a very vulnerable position due to their lack of experience and bargaining power. They may be exploited in various ways while professionally attempting to further their own career opportunities by those who do not have their best interests at heart.

This can be seen in a variety of ways, which are discussed in more detail in 'S is for Sexual Exploitation'. Exploitative people whom a model may wish to network with may offer them jobs in return for sexual favours, or for very high (or low) salaries, completely neglecting the proper recruitment process. It is one thing to gain informal work experience by professional conversation and quite another to be employed in a full-time 'job' with no experience. High incomes can trap models in jobs where they feel indebted to their boss, whereas alternatively they may be working for very little money or even for free.

It is important to assess every opportunity to understand whether it is fair and reasonable. A few days of unpaid work experience are very different to a fully blown unpaid job – assess the value that you are providing to the company and how much you are learning as a result. I once helped launch an entire business, working for free for six months because I felt too awkward to ask for payment!

If someone wishes to interview you unprofessionally (for example, at their house or a restaurant), or contacts you outside of working hours, this is a huge red flag. Do not make the mistake I have made many times of believing you can 'handle it' – predators are extremely manipulative.

For maximum safety, it is always advisable to notify your agency if you wish to gain further experience in a different field. They are there to protect you and can best advise on how to maintain professional boundaries. In the next chapter, I will show how important the role of an agency is in protecting its models, even when they are in a different country.

Anti-exploitation tips

- If someone offers you a job or other opportunity that seems too good to be true, it probably is. Refer every contact with a client outside of a booked job to your agency.
- Never, ever meet anyone at their house or another private location such as a hotel room. If you are having an informal coffee with someone, ensure it is in a public, casual location such as a cafe as opposed to at an expensive restaurant.
- Buy the person you are meeting coffee or at least pay for your own – never let anyone you are networking with buy you anything, including gifts. This avoids creating a feeling of debt.
- Always maintain professionalism and never drink alcohol, smoke or do drugs with someone you are networking with.
- If somebody makes you feel uncomfortable, very clearly tell them so. Immediately leave any situation in which you feel unsafe.
- Only contact people you are networking with during office hours (9am–6pm) and note if they try to speak to you about anything not relating to work.
- Do not allow yourself to be in vulnerable positions with people you are networking with, such as accepting a lift from them.
- Ensure that any recruitment processes go through the proper avenues (usually a human resources department if it is for a company).
- Clearly reject any sexual advances and tell your agency if this happens. Engaging in inappropriate relations to further your career will never work, and will only trap you.

is for Overseas

MODELLING IS TRULY a global job, with models being represented by agencies all over the world, catching flights to jobs on a daily basis and moving country every few months to work in a new market. Working overseas is one of the most dangerous aspects of modelling, as there is no standard recognition of how models should be treated and many models are young and vulnerable.

Travelling abroad as a model can be very lonely and scary – figuring out how to navigate a new city at the same time as trying to meet people who speak the same language as you do, let alone figuring out how to book work and be paid! The industry can be completely different in another country and it takes a while to understand, which means models can be exploited in many ways due to this vulnerability.

In this chapter, I will explain the different ways that models can work abroad and give advice on how to keep safe and avoid exploitation while overseas.

Did you know?

1. Models can travel abroad for individual jobs or be sent to live in a new country for a few months 'on stay'.

2. Models can be sent abroad with a moment's notice.

3. Models are signed to agencies abroad by their mother agency, and often do not see these contracts. They may be very unfair and include terms that breach their human rights, such as the obligation to maintain certain measurements in order to be paid.

4. Agency commission rates are different in every country – in some countries, agencies take 75% of a model's earnings!

5. Models are legally and financially responsible for their own working visas. Sometimes they may be pressured to work illegally without a visa.

6. UK-based models have to declare their foreign income. See 'T is for Tax'.

Jobs shooting abroad

Clients who are shooting abroad may bring a model out to the location. The model may be wholly dependent on the client for everything – where they sleep, what they eat, how they travel and when they work. I have been left stranded at the airport at 3am, made to sleep in a bed with a model I had never met and then worked from 6am to 10pm before!

For this reason, it is vital that agencies are fully informed and check all aspects of a job, remembering to ensure that their model is safe at all times. The model will have to take responsibility too, for example, ensuring they have all of the details physically written down – but the agency ultimately should ensure that the model is well looked after and the job is legitimate.

These jobs may be for one day or several weeks, depending on the client's requirements, and often involve a plane ride, hotel room and shoot before going back home – not the luxury travel models are assumed to enjoy. Sometimes there may be amazing perks, such as day trips or free time; my favourite job was definitely shooting in the Maldives for a week!

Usually, a model's expenses will be covered if a client has booked them on a job shooting abroad, including their food and accommodation, but this is not always the case. Models should always be fully informed whether they are expected to cover any of the costs, such as plane tickets, or if these have been 'advanced' for them.

Jobs shooting abroad may be booked by a model's mother or secondary agency – many models have foreign agencies that their mother agency contracts them to who can book them on jobs in their country (see 'A is for Agency'). If they are booked without a casting with the client, this is called a 'direct booking'. Foreign agencies normally pay a model's mother agency commission out of the total amount they take from a model's payments and they may have a separate contract agreeing this. Different foreign agencies take completely different commission amounts, which may include tax deductions. As seen in 'T is for Tax', it is important to always consult with an accountant when working abroad.

Models must ensure they have valid working visas in order to do jobs abroad – they are legally responsible for this and could be arrested if they don't have a proper visa. They can check how to do this with their agencies and should never be pressured into working illegally. Without a visa it is also much harder to be paid, as a model has no legal right to be paid money earned as a result of working illegally.

Models need to be very careful when they are booked on jobs abroad to ensure the client and job are legitimate. They can research a client online and ensure they have their contact details prior to travelling, and should never go on any jobs that they do not feel are 100% legal and safe.

Going 'on stay'

This means travelling to a new market and staying there for anywhere from a week to a year. Models commonly go on stay for periods of one to three months in new markets where they can be fresh faces, before moving on to other places. There are high seasons and different trends for different markets, so usually an agency will advise its model where to go on stay. The model will need an agency in that country, and normally will have one lined up before they arrive, or at least have appointments with agencies.

Again, models must ensure they have a valid working visa for that country and that they educate themselves about any tax obligations by speaking to their accountant before travelling. They need to be educated on all of the practicalities of working in a different country, such as the commission rates and casting processes, so they feel 100% comfortable. Usually models will travel alone to go on stay in new countries, which can be very problematic if the model is very young or vulnerable. Different laws apply to different countries and children as young as 13 have been known to model abroad by themselves!

The model is essentially moving to a new country and has no guarantee of work. They are fully responsible for all of their expenses, such as flights, rent and travel, which may be often advanced by their agency and require repayment. Debt is notoriously terrible for models travelling from place to place on stay, who may be completely financially reliant on their agencies and have a huge backlog of outstanding payments from different countries and agencies to chase, meaning they are in a constant cycle of debt as they have to borrow more money to survive. See 'E is for Expenses' for more information.

Some agencies offer models guaranteed contracts to go on stay, stating that they will definitely make a certain amount of money, as seen in 'L is for Legal'. This may be complicated by incredibly high hidden expenses such as drivers required to take models to castings, a language barrier meaning financial statements may be hard to understand and the requirement for the model to do all jobs the agency books. Such cases often breach human rights and the contracts may have very unfair terms, for example, stating that a model will not be paid if they don't maintain certain measurements and that they may have to repay the agency the guaranteed amount if they wish to leave. These are very dangerous situations to be in.

Models have to find somewhere to live when they go on stay, which can be hard if they are only there for a short time. Agencies often help them with this and may offer them a model apartment. These are notoriously horrible places to stay and the rent is usually extortionately overpriced,[39] directly profiting the agency regardless of whether the model is working. Several models often share one bedroom and I know of models who have had to sleep on the floor! Some agencies abroad even police these apartments, where models may have a nightly curfew and checks on whether

---

[39] Charles Manning, '11 horrifying ways agencies exploit their models', *Cosmopolitan*, 11 February 2016. www.cosmopolitan.com/style-beauty/fashion/news/a53455/new-model-lawsuit-agency-exploitation/. 'Models are forced to rent beds in cramped apartments owned or leased by their agencies at outrageously high rates. According to model Marcelle Almonte, in the early 2000s, her agency, MC2 Model and Talent Miami, charged her $1850 per month for a spot in a two-bedroom apartment she shared with eight other models, each paying the same rate, sleeping four to a room on bunk beds, with the last girl forced to sleep on the couch. According to the suit, the same building currently rents apartments starting at $2900 per month, meaning Almonte's agency was making as much as $13,750 more per month than today's market rate. Given that many of the models in such apartments are underage, foreign, and classified as freelancers without a steady income, it is not as if they can rent apartments on their own at a reasonable rate. And even if a young model could get a lease, her agent could decide the next day to send her to another city or country and then she would be stuck with a lease on an apartment she wasn't able to occupy.'

they have exercised! The advantages are that there are usually no rental obligations or deposits required; however, I would always advise models to stay in these apartments no longer than one week until finding accommodation of their own, independent of their agency.

It is important that models do not accept 'free' rent from club promoters who may take them clubbing in return for accommodation – more on this can be seen in 'S is for Sexual Exploitation'. The best way to find accommodation is by word of mouth between trusted friends or official short-term rental websites.

Models must always be fully informed of why their agency thinks they should go on stay in a new market and have a realistic understanding of what the market requirements are and how much money they will make. Often models may be sent to countries such as Turkey where rates of pay may be very low, but which offer a good opportunity for models to build their portfolios. They must fully understand that they may be in debt from travelling to these places, which will need to be repaid, and assess whether they actually want to go.

I insisted that I did not want to travel on stay in Europe, as I knew models were expected to be very thin and commission rates were high, nor in Asia, as I had heard that models work incredibly hard for their money there, doing up to three jobs a day. I wanted to go somewhere hot, so chose to travel to Australia to model – choosing my own career rather than allowing it to be chosen for me. Models are free to travel to any country they like and sign with an agency there if they have a valid working visa, which is a brilliant thing about the job – the freedom to travel and live almost anywhere in the world for work.

Markets are territories where models can find work. There are several different types, explained below.

- Primary markets are the biggest markets for models, with the most highly esteemed work, and so also the most competitive. Traditionally, these are London, New York, Paris and Milan.
- Secondary markets are smaller markets where models go to build experience and work for new clients. They include Barcelona, Los Angeles, Miami, Sydney, Cape Town, Hamburg, Shanghai and Tokyo.
- Tertiary markets are where many models come from or may occasionally visit for work but there is not a steady flow of constant work to justify many models living there at one time. They may include Chicago, Singapore, Hong Kong, Istanbul, Montreal, Toronto, India and Tel Aviv.

It is vital that you understand how to protect yourself while travelling abroad, as you are more vulnerable than ever when you are away from your support network of mother agency, family and friends. Personal safety, research and preparation are the necessary foundations of modelling abroad before the benefits can be enjoyed.

As we will see in the next chapter, exploitation can occur at any point in a model's life – even during a job itself – so it is vital to always understand how to protect yourself, regardless of where you are in the world.

Anti-exploitation tips

- Know all of the details before travelling abroad. Find out your accommodation, flight details and any contact details at least a few days in advance, and write them down on a piece of paper.
- Ask your agency to see any contracts relating to foreign work or agencies BEFORE they are signed (these would involve booking agreements, as seen in 'L is for Legal'). Always have a lawyer or Equity read foreign contracts and ensure you fully understand them, remembering that your agency will negotiate contracts on your behalf if you wish.

- You do not have to join an agency chosen for you or travel abroad if you don't want to. You can travel to a country and visit agencies yourself if you wish to do so.
- When you join a foreign agency, ensure that you find out about all of their payment practices, expenses systems and commission rates. Educate yourself on how your money will be processed and how you will receive it before going! Ask you foreign agency for a recommendation of an industry-specialised accountant in that country to visit when you arrive.
- Speak to your accountant before working abroad in any new country and find out whether you need any forms that will exempt you from having unnecessary tax automatically deducted from your payments. See 'T is for Tax'.
- Always stay in control of your passport. Some agencies may take your passport when you arrive for 'processing' purposes. Never let them keep your passport overnight, and insist on them taking copies as opposed to keeping the original document. Ensure you have both a printed-out scan of your passport and a virtual scan on your phone when travelling.
- ALWAYS ensure that you have a visa. Some agencies encourage models to work without a visa – even legitimate, highly established agencies. It does not make a difference to them if you are barred from the country or end up in prison. You may also need a visa if you are shooting a job abroad, which you should check with your agency and accountant. Always make sure you have the legal right to work and stay in a country before visiting.
- Educate yourself on how to leave the agency and the country in case of an emergency. Always keep enough money in your bank account to pay for a plane ticket home.
- Establish where you will live before you travel anywhere new, knowing the address at least a month in advance. Ask on social media if any friends have any accommodation recommendations in new countries.
- Learn some words in the language, take out some foreign currency in advance and educate yourself on the transport

system. Write down emergency phone numbers and the address of your home country's consulate in case of emergency.

- Buy a phone plan that offers international roaming or ensure you buy a local SIM card before leaving the airport. Always make sure that you have 3G, credit and a fully charged phone. You should always have a phone charger with you, and a foreign plug adaptor.
- Always have worldwide travel insurance.
- Use an international credit card to reduce high exchange fees.
- Always know your bank details, including SWIFT and IBAN codes and anything else required for a foreign payment.
- Avoid getting into any debt. Agencies often offer cash advances to models on stay with them so that they can afford to live. It is never advisable take these, as interest can be added and the expenses are extremely hard to keep track of and question, especially if it is with a new agency. See 'E is for Expenses'.
- Never allow a foreign agency to pay you in cash or encourage you to break the law. Payments should go through your bank and you should have proper receipts of work, such as a financial statement.
- Stay safe by undertaking self-defence classes and have a basic understanding of street safety, such as hiding money in different places on your body (such as cash in your socks!) and never being on your phone carelessly in public. Research dangerous areas of the city you will be in and make sure you avoid them, taking taxis where possible.
- Ensure that you take the time to recover from lack of sleep and look after yourself properly. Eat three sustainable meals per day and always have snacks and water with you. Make sure that you know the policy on tap water – if in doubt, do not drink it.
- Avoid running and walking outside at night. If you would like to exercise, make use of your accommodation, such as

taking a skipping rope in your suitcase or doing an online fitness class.

- Always avoid clubbing, alcohol, drugs and club promoters. Remember that there is no such thing as a free lunch and club promoters may target lonely models for their own profit. See 'S is for Sexual Exploitation'.

- Make friends by asking on social media if any friends have connections in the country you are visiting, or ask your agency to connect you with any models that would be willing to get a coffee with you, especially those who speak the same language. Look for social activities such as language exchange lessons that are featured online.

is for Posing

POSING IS THE essence of modelling, the magic models perform in front of the camera as they connect all of the visions in the room and breathe life into them. This opens them up to a certain level of vulnerability, to criticism and control by others.

The more work you do as a model, the more comfortable you will become in front of a camera. It can be quite intimidating on set, with sometimes up to 20 cameras pointed at you and a room filled with people watching how you will perform, as you try to take on several opinions to do the best job possible. Posing is a lot of pressure.

Many models are exploited on jobs through 'posing' instructions in the dubious name of art, by people who can manipulate them into doing things they feel uncomfortable with. The relationship between a photographer and model on set is extremely intimate, where the model is very vulnerable, following instructions and trying to please the photographer.

In this chapter, I will demonstrate how posing can be used to exploit models and how they can protect themselves against this, empowering themselves to do the best job possible. It ultimately comes down to being able to understand the difference between creativity and exploitation.

Did you know?

1. Sometimes models will be given advice on how to pose by a photographer and other times they may be given no advice at all.

2. Most professional models receive no training in how to pose, and learn on the job.

3. Often, models will be spoken about by various people on jobs as though they are not present.

4. Models may be asked to pose at castings and on jobs.

How to pose professionally

As a model, you should always be made to feel comfortable on a job by the team. Normally, a photographer will help you to 'warm up' by explaining what kind of poses are required and what mood the client wants while giving you instructions during shooting. By being prepared and understanding what is expected of you, you can ensure that you are confident that you are doing a good job and are not vulnerable.

The below are examples of professional conduct relating to making a model feel comfortable whilst posing on a job.

- Being introduced to everyone on set and always being provided with a private changing room, a suitable dressing gown to cover up between shots and proper breaks.
- Being provided with food and drink.
- Speaking to other models on the day or acquainting yourself with any props you might have to use.

- Understanding what different pieces of equipment and people do on a job – ask them!
- Being spoken to and treated with respect at all times by everyone on the job.
- Showing certain facial expressions, such as smiling or looking a certain way. If you are told to 'smile with your eyes', a helpful tip is to think about a very happy memory while looking into the camera.
- Breathing through your mouth. This is a good base pose for models to know and helps them to relax and focus on their breathing.
- Squinting. A slightly odd one but often recommended for high-fashion modelling, along with furrowing your eyebrows to look serious.
- Relaxing parts of your body, such as your shoulders or the famous 'claw hands' many models get. Models are often told to relax when they are looking stiff and uncomfortable.
- Showing your best angles, which means the most photogenic angles of your face. Models can work these out by asking their agency or the photographer.
- Showing a range of expressions and poses in very short amounts of time. It is good to do this by naturally blending movements into one another. Many YouTube videos show how models do this.
- Playing with your hair, walking around the set, crossing your arms, pretending to hold a pea with your index fingers and thumbs and working with the clothes, using the pockets.
- Copying a pose from the photographer or following instructions that you feel comfortable with.
- Interacting with other models or props on the shoot, as long as you feel comfortable.

How posing can be exploitative

Unfortunately, as modelling is an artistic job with no proper guidelines and involving a lot of 'creatives', many models may be exploited under the guise of art.[40] Essentially this means models do things they are not comfortable with because they believe they are required for the job, are standard practice for models or because they are simply being creative as opposed to being manipulated. They may have much older, more experienced people telling them to pose in certain ways or relaxing them using very unprofessional methods such as massages or drugs, which should never happen on a job. Ways that the concept of posing can be used to exploit models are further discussed in 'S is for Sexual Exploitation' and can also include the below conduct by anyone on a job relating to you as a model.

- Offering you drugs, alcohol or cigarettes.
- Joking about sex or other inappropriate topics with you.
- Doing breathing or relaxation exercises with you that can induce a state of hypnosis or extreme vulnerability.
- Touching you in any way that makes you feel uncomfortable, such as massages or pinching your nipples to make them hard.
- Intentionally causing a reaction, such as provoking you into being shocked.
- Stating that your agency has given permission for something in advance and so you have to do it. Always double-check this and remember you can always say no, even if they have said yes!
- Being told to do something you do not feel comfortable with, such as posing provocatively or kissing someone.
- Pressuring you to shoot nudity or underwear. Intentionally luring you into a false sense of comfort by suggesting you take down your bra straps, then take off your top, then bra and cover your nipples. This is done a lot on jobs and is

---

[40] Jacob Bernstein, Matthew Schneier and Vanessa Friedman, 'Male models say Mario Testino and Bruce Weber sexually exploited them', *The New York Times*, 13 January 2018. www.nytimes.com/2018/01/13/style/mario-testino-bruce-weber-harassment.html; 'For a fashion model, success is the ability to incite desire. The job requirements often include nudity and feigning seduction; provocation is a lever for sales… Models were asked to breathe and to touch both themselves and [the photographer], moving their hands wherever they felt their "energy."'

intentionally aimed to make the model feel comfortable and results in them being exploited, shooting something they do not want to shoot.

- Lying to you to get you to do something you don't want to do, for example, stating that your nipples will be edited out later or the images will be taken from a certain point. These are strangers who ultimately cannot be trusted to do what they say.
- Speaking about you as though you are not there, especially in a degrading or humiliating way.

Anti-exploitation tips

- If you ever feel unsafe on a job, leave immediately and phone your agency.
- Understand exactly what is expected of you on a job. Your agency should tell you what a job involves beforehand; however, they may not always give you all of the details. Ask them for a 'booking agreement' (see 'L is for Legal'), call sheet and mood board when you are booked for a job.
- Ask clients during castings what the job will involve and what they are looking for in a model. See 'Q is for Questions'.
- Ask the client upon arrival what the day will include and tell them if you do not feel comfortable with anything as soon as possible.
- Ask to see the mood board when you arrive to a job, which will have the inspiration for the shots the clients would like. Ask them what kind of style/energy they would like from you before you start shooting.
- Feel empowered to say no to anything at all, especially work involving nudity, underwear, swimwear, kissing other models and dangerous props such as motorbikes.
- Research the client before a casting or job to see what kind of poses the models on their websites are doing and practise these at home.
- Never accept any drugs, alcohol or cigarettes from anyone on a job.

is for Questions

Models often feel very intimidated to work with so many professional adults at such a young age and can be very shy to ask questions, which in turn results in exploitation as they do not use their voice. People are not mind-readers and if they don't know how a model is feeling, they can't help them – by asking questions models can ensure they are heard and respected.

There is so much that is simply assumed about models, such as the fact that they know how to get paid by their agency – I wasn't paid for six months because I had no idea I had to ask the accountant if any money had arrived for me! Especially with agencies that take on experienced models who assume that the models know everything about the industry and they do not have to explain it to them, when this is often not the case and every agency works completely differently. Clients usually assume the model knows everything about a job that their agency does, which is rarely the case.

Due to intimidating situations, models may be afraid to ask questions or speak out if they feel uncomfortable, which results in negative effects for everyone on set as the model is not feeling comfortable. In this chapter, I will demonstrate how to make conversation with professionals you may come into contact with as a model and how to ensure your voice is heard. These are all valid questions that deserve to be answered.

Did you know?

1. On a job, models have no say in how they look. People will start working on their hair, make-up and clothes possibly without telling them what they are doing or how the model will look.

2. Models often have absolutely no idea what a job involves before turning up on the day; however, everyone on set assumes that they have received the information and that they understand what is required of them.

3. Models often work with very successful adults and are usually the youngest people on a job.

4. Models often don't find out about a job until 6pm the evening before.

Questions to ask your agency

Your agency is accountable for all information about your career that you would like to know – you are paying them money to work for you. More transparency is needed, especially in terms of models knowing what their agency is doing for them, details of jobs and their schedules. You should feel empowered to ask any of the questions below, and any others that you would like to know the answer to.

• How does this agency work? Can you send me all of the information you would normally send to a brand-new model?

By asking your agency to explain how their procedures work, who your bookers are, how and when you will be paid and for any benefits that new models may receive, you are reminding them that you are not all-knowing. Even if you have modelled with a different agency, everyone works differently and this is something that is often forgotten.

- How much commission do you take?

Ask your agency to very clearly and transparently explain their commission system to you, including any agency fees they charge to the client and money taken from your payment.

- How do you verify clients and photographers?

It is important that your agency knows who they are sending you to work with are trustworthy and professional people.

- Can you introduce me to other models/send me on castings/ to test shoots with other models?

Your agency can easily line up your schedule with other models to ensure that you are not alone. You can always take a chaperone to any work you feel uncomfortable with and never have to attend anything alone.

- Can you ensure that I am not sent to private houses/hotel rooms?

Many castings and shoots take place in the houses of clients and photographers, which a model should never have to attend – especially not alone.

- Can you send me how my schedule looks a week in advance?

Your agent should easily be able to do this for you every week if you remind them via email. It is very helpful to know the castings, options and jobs you are holding for the next week.

- How is my schedule looking?

This is helpful to do via telephone at any time during working hours if you want to know how the next few days look.

- Can I book out?

  You can always book out any time you like and do not have to give a reason, although you will often be asked for one. I always say that I am seeing family – your agency are not entitled to know what you are doing in your private life.

- Can you help me with X?

  Your agency is there to support and guide you throughout your career. If you are struggling with anything at all such as health issues, or want to develop your career more in a certain area, ask your agent for an appointment to discuss this. That is what you are paying them for!

- What do you see for me in the upcoming months?

  It's good to schedule in a regular chat with your agent to discuss your career as a whole. They can share with you any feedback from clients and strategies to book more work, such as travelling abroad.

- What are the full details (including the permitted usages, call sheet, mood board and payment rates) of this job?

  Some agents will only send the model the very basic information they need to know, such as an address and time. Particularly if you are shooting on location, it is good to receive the full call sheet detailing all locations and contact numbers.

- How do you book jobs and can I see my booking form?

  Agents often sign contracts on behalf of models with the client when they are booked on jobs that detail how the images are allowed to be used and any extra terms such as social media restrictions. Models should always be allowed to see these at any time, but most have no idea that they exist!

This may be because the agency does not want the model to see the contact details of the client or the gross rate of pay including the agency fee charged to the client.

- Can I see my contract?

  You are entitled to see any contract involving you at any time you like, including those that your agency has signed on your behalf with foreign agencies.

- Why am I not working/how can I work more?

  If you haven't had any work in a couple of weeks, ask your agent for a meeting to discuss why. It might just be a quiet time in general, or there may be a problem specifically with you, such as being overworked in that market. This reminds your agent that you are keen to work.

- Can you propose me to this client/sign me with an agency in this country?

  By telling your agency what you want from them, they can work for you instead of doing what they think is best.

- Who is the agency accountant?

  The accountant is not always obvious and may be hidden in a separate area of the agency. It is very important to speak to them in order to understand about your finances with the agency.

- Can you send me my images?

  After doing a photoshoot you may have to wait for several weeks or months until the images are published. The client may send your agent the images to use in your portfolio, but they will not automatically send them on to you, so it is important to ask your agent for these to be sent to you. You will need them if you want to change agency in the future.

Questions to ask your agency accountant

- Can we have a meeting?

  Sit down with the accountant and ask them to fully explain all of the agency's finance procedures, such as methods of payment and financial statements.

- What is an agency account? Can you ensure you never use this without my permission?

  They will explain to you how the model account system works, which you should always avoid using. Tell them expressly, in writing, that you do not allow them to charge expenses without asking for your permission first.

- Do you charge an 'advance fee' or any interest rates? Do you have a financial licence to do this?

  Check that your agency is not charging you any hidden fees. If they are paying you before a client pays them and charging you interest, they will usually need a financial licence for this too, which can easily be checked online.

- How long will it take for me to be paid?

  All agencies work differently; however, in the UK they must legally pay a model within ten working days of receiving their money from a client. Check with your accountant every week for any money that has been paid for you and ask them how long certain clients usually take to pay.

- Can I have a financial statement?

  This is good to have every month and especially relevant for filing your tax return at the end of the year. It will list the jobs that have been paid to you and any expenses that have been charged. You can also ask for a list of any outstanding payments.

- Can I have a receipt for/what are these expenses?

  Often random expenses will appear on a model's financial statement and it is important to always check these with your agency. UK agencies should not usually charge for any in-house marketing fees, such as appearing on a website, or 'courier' fees. They should always be able to provide you with a receipt or invoice for any expenses charged, such as for a test shoot.

- How do buy-outs work?

  Ask the accountant to explain how you will find out if a client has paid for extra usage of your images. They should normally inform you, but you may have to email them to ask!

- Have I been paid?

  You may have to ask if any money has been paid by clients to you in order to receive that money. It is a good idea to send a monthly email to your accountant asking if they have received any payments for you. After leaving an agency, email them twice a year to check if you have been paid any extra fees for work done in the past.

Questions to ask a client at a casting

- What are you casting for?

  This opens up a dialogue of conversation, which shows you are interested in the job itself.

- Where/when are you shooting?

  This is good to know in advance and allows the client to subconsciously imagine you as the model for the job. It also prepares you, as seen in 'K is for Knowing What to Expect'.

- What kind of model are you looking for?

It is advisable to ask the client what they are looking for in the model that they book, because it will give you an opportunity to sell yourself. If they want a model with lots of personality, you can tell them about all of your hobbies - or if they are looking for a model with a great deal of experience, you can tell them about previous clients you have worked for.

- How has your day been?

There is often silence while a client looks at your portfolio and this is always a good filler question.

Questions to ask a client on a job

- What are you going to do with these pictures?

Clients agree the usage of a shoot's images with the model agency; however, sometimes the model does not know how they will be used. I asked this on my first shoot and was told they would be published in *Vogue*! It is also good to be aware in case the client goes outside of their agreed usage terms and owes you more money (royalties) as a result. See 'L is for Legal'.

- When will these images be out?

You can stay informed of when the images will be published by asking the client. You can also ask the client to send you the images via social media if your agency does not send them to you.

- Can I have your email address?

It is good to have a contact email address for a client just in case you have an issue with payment later on. If your agency says they haven't paid, but you think they have, you can check this with the client themselves. Avoid emailing the client unless strictly necessary and never with regards to working directly with them (without the use of your agency) as this is likely breaking your agency contract and you have no guarantee that the client will pay you.

- Can I see the mood board?

By seeing the inspiration shots you can understand what a client wants from you.

- How many outfits do we have to shoot?

It is good to have a rough idea of how much you have to shoot, and how quick each photograph needs to be taken in order to finish.

- When is lunch?

Clients should always provide models with a lunch break and with a nutritious, healthy lunch.

- Can I have a break?

Clients often don't realise how tiring modelling can be, and they would prefer you to have a rest rather than look tired and exhausted in the shots.

- Do you have a heater?

Often jobs may be in very cold temperatures, even if they are indoors. Clients will sometimes have heaters in their studio to keep models warm if needed.

- Where is my changing room?

You should always have privacy to change on a job.

Questions to ask the team on a job

- Has this brush been cleaned?

It is important that dirty hair and make-up brushes are not used on models, as infections can easily be caught this way.

- Has this dressing gown been washed?

Models are often given dressing gowns to wear on set; however, sometimes these may be very unhygienic to wear if they haven't been washed, which is best to ask the fashion stylist on a job. It is advisable to take along your own.

- What products are you using? Can you use my products instead?

Hair and make-up artists should respect a model's wishes, especially if they have allergies.

- What kind of skin/hair do I have? How can I best look after it?

It is helpful to learn insider secrets and understand your body.

- Can you please stop hurting me?

Hair stylists are notorious for brushing, backcombing and overheating models' hair within an inch of its life. Make-up artists can also sometimes cause pain by curling a model's eyelashes and stylists can steam clothes while models are wearing them. They often do not realise they are hurting models so it's important to tell them!

- Do you have any heat protector?

Hair stylists generally have heat protector, but fail to use it in the haste of getting their job done.

- Can you take this out of my hair/off my skin?

Some jobs require especially wacky hairstyles or make-up looks, which can be quite embarrassing and hard to remove.

- Should I hang up the clothes?

A stylist will always remember if you ask this and really appreciate it – there is nothing worse than picking clothes up off the floor after a model!

- Do you offer complimentary treatments or products in return for social media postings?

This is a bold question to ask but it is very, very worth it!

- What is your Instagram account?

  As seen in 'I is for Instagram', it is good practice to tag/credit everyone involved in a job on any images you may post on social media afterwards. It is also a good way of networking for future work. More on this can be found in 'N is for Networking'.

Be inquisitive about everything around you and hold everyone accountable for their jobs – don't stay the passive human mannequin because it suits other people. By respecting yourself, you teach others to do the same, reminding them that you are a real person with real feelings, not an object. As we will see in the next chapter, this is the inherent problem with modelling, as models are often treated as inanimate objects. It is very easy for people who are profiting off your modelling services to forget that you are a human being and are affected by the things they do and say.

Anti-exploitation tips

- Be confident when speaking to others and maintain eye contact.
- If you are ignored, ask again. If you are still ignored (for example, some of my bookers have had a tendency to ignore any emails they didn't want to answer!), speak to someone else (such as a head booker) and let them know what has happened.
- If someone does something you do not feel comfortable with, tell them this and speak to your agency as soon as possible. They are there to stand up for you.
- Never compromise with your health, safety and wellbeing. If someone is making you feel unsafe, tell them politely that you feel that way.
- If you are intimidated on a job, find the most friendly looking person and ask them anything you like. They will be able to speak to others on set for you.

is for Rejection

THE NUMBER-ONE WORD you will hear as a model is 'NO'. Every single model has been rejected throughout their career, no matter how successful they may be today.

Rejection makes up about 90% of modelling. Models have to be incredibly strong to withstand this constant rejection, to understand that it isn't a personal issue and to build a thick skin. This is a natural part of life; however, the way that models are rejected can often be very degrading and seriously impact their long-term mental health. Exploitation commonly occurs as vulnerable models desperately seek acceptance by others, as can be seen in 'S is for Sexual Exploitation'.

In this chapter, I will show how models experience rejection and how to deal with it in a healthy way.

Did you know?

1. Models have to attend roughly 15 castings in order to book one job.

2. Models can be sent home from a job if the client doesn't like them on the day. I have seen this happen a few times!

3. Rejection can come in many forms, from almost every single person a model works with.

How models can be rejected

From the very beginning of your career as a model, you will be rejected when applying to join model agencies, who often have too many models on their books and are looking for something undefinably unique in a model. There is no maximum number of models that an agency can have and often they simply have too many to look after properly.

This may happen after you have been scouted by an agency, which is extremely difficult if you have no experience of the industry – you may have your hopes up and tell many people, thinking this is a sign you have what it takes to become a model, only to be brutally rejected to your face. You may be made to wait for hours or days before being told a firm answer, are rarely given feedback and can even be laughed at, as happened to a friend of mine after walking into an agency that had scouted her! Similarly, if you walk into an agency or apply online, due to the sheer volume of applications they receive (see 'A is for Agency'), it is highly unlikely that you will be accepted.

This rejection is often take to mean 'you aren't good enough'. It is normal to project your own insecurities onto the rejection, developing serious mental health issues or eating disorders as a result of being rejected by a stranger. It is always an incredibly demoralising and humiliating process to be rejected to your face.

The prospect of being rejected by your agency continues all the way through your career, being scrutinised by your bookers every time you walk into the agency for possible signs of weight gain or issues such as skin problems. I have been shouted at when visiting my agency for putting an inch on my waist and told that I would be taken off a very highly paid, confirmed job because of this!

This fear is something that is constantly hanging over models' heads, as their agency can stop representing them with no notice. Friends of mine have received their images in the post with no prior warning that they were being dropped! Agents can also simply telephone or email you with the news that you are no longer being represented by them.

This is an incredibly scary thought, as models have no protection – they can essentially be fired at any time (despite being self-employed!), under the pressure to be perfect at all times. Unfortunately, for many models the acceptance by their agency equates to their self-worth and they feel a strong sense of loyalty to those who may feel none at all towards them. Modelling is ultimately a business and, nice as your bookers may be, they are doing their jobs and work comes first. Models are essentially products to be sold and consideration of their feelings is extra work for some bookers.

Castings are also met with rejection most of the time, with models putting in serious effort travelling to many castings per day only to not book any work due to the intense competition of the industry – in my experience booking roughly 1 in 20 castings. Feedback is not usually given at castings; however, models usually try to decipher how they went by overthinking them later on. Whether they were asked try on clothes, how much attention was given to other models, how friendly the client was or how quickly they were seen are all common anxieties for models. By overthinking castings they either build themselves up for potential disappointment or unfairly punish themselves, when usually there is absolutely no way to tell how a casting went or if a client likes you. Usually, the ones I think went the worst were the ones I ended up booking!

There are usually very long queues at castings unless a model has been 'requested' specifically by a client, as seen in 'C is for Castings'. Models will usually spend at least one hour getting ready, one to two hours in total travelling to and from a casting and at least ten minutes of waiting time (usually closer to one hour), all to be seen for a matter of minutes. I have waited for hours in casting queues only to be told to leave as soon as I walked in and have heard every negative comment possible about myself by strangers during castings over the years. It simply is an industry where you cannot win, and you need to develop a thick enough skin to withstand this. I developed depersonalisation to cope and did not see my body as my own after years of objectification, resulting in further problems, such as depression. More on the mental health effects of rejection can be seen in 'Z is for Zen'.

Models are optioned for jobs before being confirmed (usually the night before), which means that even when they are shortlisted for work, they may not be booked. Clients can even cancel jobs once they have been confirmed, which leaves models on a constant rollercoaster of hope and rejection. Imagine being optioned for thousands of pounds of work and never booking it!

Even during a job, models can be rejected at any point throughout the day! Clients often send models home if they don't like how they look or if they don't fit the clothes properly. This is extremely upsetting to go through and models may even not be paid for turning up to work, and so are punished for something that is not their fault. The client should have responsibility when booking the model to ensure they are suitable for the job, which is why castings exist.

Models can also be rejected while shooting – I have often been asked to wait out while the other model shoots swimwear after both of us had started shooting. I literally sat there comparing myself and trying to understand why I was not good enough to shoot swimwear, scrutinising every hushed word and conversation, feeling very self-conscious, which impacted the rest of the day.

Models are often spoken about as though they are not there by the team on a job and may be treated with general disrespect, often being expected to do things they do not want to do. Due to the lack of transparency, models often do not know what their agency and the client has agreed to and may be misled into feeling guilty and 'difficult' if they say no to something such as shooting nudity. I have had this experience many times myself.

Even after doing a job, models can still be rejected. I have had clients that didn't use the images they shot of me for a billboard campaign, reshooting it on another model. I had told everyone I knew I would be on billboards and saw this campaign every day, a constant reminder that I was not good enough with no explanation as to why. Models can even be told that they will not be paid for their work after doing it, as I once was because the client apparently 'didn't like how I suited their clothes', despite them still using the pictures and cutting my face off! Agencies often don't act in these situations because they want to protect their relationships with clients.

Experiencing constant rejection can lead to serious mental health issues, as seen in 'Z is for Zen'. We are often our own worst critics and insecurity is often in our heads, as there is a complete lack of honest communication. It is important for models to understand how often they will be rejected and whether they want to put themselves through this as a routine part of their job.

Being 'difficult'

Models tend to be very agreeable and people-pleasing due to the constant threat of rejection from different people every day. It is a common theme among models to fear being deemed 'difficult to work with' by clients or agencies – in other words, to upset anybody, because these people have the power of your career in their hands. This is what in turn leads to models being exploited and abused as they feel embarrassed to speak up for themselves and potentially close themselves off to any future work.

This is a terrible way to live your life, as it is very hard to switch off. I sought out acceptance from every single person in my life and could not feel happy within myself, similarly to many other models I know. Models are notorious for having difficult relationships as they seek endless acceptance from their partners who usually have their own misconceptions about how confident models are!

It is hardly surprising that models feel this way, as their life is being held by strings that could be cut at any time. Negative feedback from one client could upset their agency and mean the model is penalised, with work being withheld from them as a result.[41]

Some models I know have been threatened by clients and photographers that they would give bad feedback if the models didn't do what they wanted (such as shooting nudity). I will demonstrate how this happens in more detail in the next chapter, showing how the precarious position of models is often used to exploit them sexually.

Anti-exploitation tips

- Do not take anything personally, as rejection is very rarely for the reasons you assume. Remember that for the client, you are a product. They are thinking about their business, not your feelings.

---

[41] Charles Manning, '11 horrifying ways agencies exploit their models', *Cosmopolitan*, 11 February 2016. www.cosmopolitan.com/style-beauty/fashion/news/a53455/new-model-lawsuit-agency-exploitation/. 'When models push back against their agents and demand transparency and a proper reckoning of their wages, they are punished. Barker claims that when she pressed her agency about a big check she was supposed to have received… her agency blackballed her by telling photographers who requested her for other jobs that she was all booked up and unavailable to work, despite the fact that she had no work at all.'

- Do not be afraid to be 'difficult' and stand up for yourself. Those who would treat you badly for this do not deserve to work with you in the first place. Respect yourself enough to walk away from anything that does not serve you.
- Remember that no one has the right to treat you with disrespect. If you feel uncomfortable staying on a job, call your agency, who should support you. Differentiate between behaviour that is careless or rude and that which is unprofessional and disrespectful.
- Weigh up every situation carefully. I usually leave situations that I do not think will benefit me, such as waiting for three hours to be seen at a casting. This comes with self-confidence and respect.
- Have a strong sense of self. By having a healthy appreciation for yourself it will be harder for others' opinions to hurt you as you do not rely on them for happiness. Write down things that you like about yourself every day.
- Expect nothing, appreciate everything. It is best to assume you have not booked any jobs until you receive the confirmation email. Appreciate every experience as a lesson, teaching you something new.
- Stay polite but strong. If you experience rudeness or rejection from someone, politely say that the way they are acting is unnecessarily upsetting. They often may not realise how their actions make you feel, and rude people are usually having a bad day.
- Ask your agency for feedback; they will be able to reassure you about the reasons for any rejection.
- Practice self-love. Read your favourite books, dance to your favourite music, eat your favourite food and spend time making yourself happy, whether that is by bubble baths or seeing people you love. See more in 'Z is for Zen'.
- Find your identity outside of modelling. Discover your passions and what interests you, what you can 'do' when you aren't working. Write down every single thing that makes you feel happy and start doing it – you don't need anyone's

permission to educate yourself or start a new hobby. Even better if these things can potentially bring you some stable income!

- Save your money – don't be lulled into a false sense of security by regular work, as it can end suddenly. See 'F is for Finance'.
- Remember that you don't have to model. Be confident enough to know you will happily survive if you aren't a model, and you can leave the industry at any time.

is for Sexual Exploitation

MODELS ARE VERY vulnerable people who are open to constant sexual exploitation. With short career spans, an oversupply of models and a dwindling amount of work, models are always looking to someone else to help further their career. They have very intimate, informal working practices, in close contact with strangers who have enormous amounts of power over them. The scarcity of work often means that models may find themselves in financial problems and be targeted by exploitative predators.

Almost every single model that I know has suffered some form of sexual exploitation. It is often normalised in the fashion industry, passed off as jokes and creativity, but it isn't acceptable. Sexual exploitation comes in various forms, not just pressures involving nudity, as seen in 'X is for X-Rated', but also general control and abuse in all aspects of a model's life for the sexual gratification of another person.

In this chapter, I will explain how models can recognise potentially sexually exploitative situations and how to avoid danger. It is important for models to be members of Equity (see 'U is for Unionising'), who offer free independent advice and legal support to their members.

Did you know?

1. When surveyed, 76.5% of models said they have been exposed to drugs and/or alcohol on the job.[42]

2. Models are often in vulnerable positions and may be expected to undress in front of strangers; 60.5% of surveyed models said their lack of privacy while changing clothes is a major concern.[43]

3. Inappropriate touching on the job was experienced by 29.7% of surveyed models and 28% had been pressured to have sex with someone at work.[44]

4. Models may be taken out for free dinner and alcohol any night of the week by club promoters.

5. Some models have been offered money in return for sex.

Sexual exploitation by an agency

As gatekeepers of their models' careers, agencies have a great deal of power. Offending your bookers could mean not being able to pay rent next month – and models are all competing to be pushed for work by their bookers. Although bookers should treat their models equally and with respect, sometimes this may be affected by their personal motivations.

The line between personal and professional boundaries is often blurred – bookers generally know what their models are doing at all times and can send them on work they do not want to

---

[42] The Model Alliance, '2012 Industry Survey, Industry Analysis'. http://modelalliance.org/industry-analysis
[43] Ibid.
[44] Ibid.

do, even calling them back off holiday. Bookers may often use unprofessional language such as 'babe', 'darling' and 'honey', which can be ironic – especially if this is while telling a model to lose weight! One agency I had forced me to air kiss all the bookers every time I saw them, telling me off if I forgot.

This blur leaves models wide open to sexual exploitation by those who are supposed to protect them. Especially when alcohol, drugs or sex is involved, these lines become non-existent and models are at the complete mercy of their bookers. Both models and bookers should be educated about what a healthy professional relationship looks like and strong boundaries need to be enforced.

Sexual exploitation by a model agency is not limited to, but could include:

- Treating models in any way that makes them feel uncomfortable, including inappropriate touching, language, actions or suggestions.
- Any sexual behaviour with their model, especially in terms of dating them.
- Pressurising models into doing any kind of work they do not want to do, especially of a sexual nature.
- Not properly checking who they are sending models to meet and work with.
- Consciously sending models to work with dangerous people.
- Not asking the permission of the model or informing them about anything they may feel uncomfortable doing before confirming work, such as shooting lingerie or having to kiss another model
- Not supporting their models when told about exploitation.
- Providing their models with drugs or alcohol or opportunities where these may be offered to them.
- Encouraging models to attend events outside of work; care should always be taken to ensure that events are strictly professional and that the agency is not being paid for models' attendance.

- Inviting models to spend time outside of the office with agency staff members alone.
- Sending models on jobs or castings that are not legitimate.
- Unhealthy contact with a model, sharing too much of their professional life or asking too much about the models' lives; contact outside of typical working hours (9am–6pm) should be heavily monitored.

Other forms of inappropriate conduct by an agency are not limited to, but could include:

- Imposing any obligations on the model that are not strictly required for their work, such as a curfew.
- Asking for money or gifts from a model.
- Speaking about or to a model disrespectfully or consistently ignoring them.
- Not supporting a model who is visibly suffering.
- Financial exploitation of a model, for example, by excessive spending on their behalf or encouraging them to accept personal loans.
- Encouraging a model to act illegally, such as encouraging them to work abroad without a visa or to take drugs to lose weight.
- Not verifying foreign agencies and contracts.
- Encouraging a model to act unhealthily, for example, by not eating!
- Pressurising a model to do any work they do not want to do, such as shooting with fur.
- Negligence regarding a model, such as booking them on dangerous jobs where they may be injured and not properly organising their care, for example, transport and food.
- Bullying a model, for example, talking about them in front of them as though they are not there, whispering about them, laughing at them and not treating them as a human being.
- Pressurising a model to stay in certain accommodation (especially if the bookers live there themselves) or accept expenses such as a driver.

Sexual exploitation at work

Sexual exploitation is common during castings and jobs due to the expendable nature of models. Working environments may often be very informal and intimate, where clients have enormous power over models – they have literally hired them out for a day and models are hesitant to say no in fear of being reported as 'difficult' to their agency, as seen in 'R is for Rejection'.

There is currently no standard way of checking if a client is safe for models to work with. Work can be anywhere from a hotel room to a house, involve anything from dancing in underwear to kissing another model. It is normal practice for strangers to request to photograph models in their underwear or ask them to change in front of them, whether they are on a casting or a job – but this doesn't mean it is right. Clients can ask a model to do anything at all, including posing naked, and if a model doesn't feel comfortable enough to say no this may affect their entire life.

Models under the age of 18 may be advised to have a chaperone, which may not be effective enough if their chaperone doesn't recognise what is unacceptable behaviour. I was literally laughed at when telling men I felt uncomfortable as they saw me almost completely naked at the age of 13, and my mum was in the next room. Models are usually dressed on shoots by other people, to protect the clothes from make-up and creasing; however, this should not be accepted as the norm. It isn't okay for someone to feel entitled to see anyone else naked, regardless of their profession or background. Models are rarely given private changing areas and I have had my photograph taken without my permission several times while changing backstage at fashion shows.

Sexual exploitation on a job is not limited to, but could include:

- Anybody treating a model inappropriately, physically or not, making them feel uncomfortable; any kind of sexual assault, from touching to rape.

- People touching a model under a 'legitimate' reasoning such as applying moisturising lotion without obtaining prior permission.
- Making sexual comments, suggestions or actions involving a model.
- Anybody pressurising a model to do something they do not want to do, especially if they haven't been informed about it prior to arriving at the job or casting; this can involve shooting nudity, swimwear or lingerie, kissing another person or posing in a certain way.
- Grooming of models to make them feel comfortable; persuading them to accept massages, alcohol, drugs or cigarettes.
- Grooming of models to undress if they have refused, such as taking down straps and posing in their bra, then 'covering' themselves.
- Depriving models of a private changing area and asking them to change in public.
- Not giving models the option to change by themselves and appointing them a 'dresser'.
- Offering models work in return for sexual favours.
- Filming models during a job when it has not been agreed by an agency, especially if it involves underwear/swimwear; obviously, any secret filming is illegal but does happen so it is important for a model to check out a location thoroughly upon arrival for any suspicious lights.
- Harassment of models during and after a job, contacting them directly in any way that is unprofessional.
- Pressuring a model to wear something they do not want to wear, especially if it is sheer/see-through.
- Photographing/filming models changing.
- Spiking models with drugs.
- Not giving models proper care with regards to sleeping arrangements, for example, making them share a bed/bedroom with other people without their informed consent.

Other exploitation on a job may include, but is not limited to:

- Pressurising models to work even when they are clearly unwell/exhausted.
- Extreme working situations, where they are not given breaks/lunch/water and have to shoot excessive amounts of clothes.
- Demeaning a model in any way, for example, pressurising them to shoot something that humiliates them, such as in my case having elastic bands wrapped around my face and neck for an hour!
- Pressurising models to do something they do not want to do, such as working with fur or animals, irrespective of what has been agreed with the agency.
- Injuring a model by negligence, for example, by burning them with a hair straightener.
- Dangerous working conditions (especially if there is no insurance taken out for the model) such as work with motorbikes and in abandoned buildings.
- Extreme working conditions such as excessively hot/cold temperatures without taking proper care of the model; I once shot fur coats all day in 40-degree heat!
- Negligence regarding the model, for example, I was once stranded at an airport at 3am because transport had not been organised for me!

Sexual exploitation by promoters

There is a dark undercurrent of sexual exploitation outside the boundaries of a model's professional life, which becomes very complicated as they have even less protection in these situations where their agencies have no power. Models may often be invited out to free lunches, dinners and nights out with club promoters who financially profit off their presence.[45]

These people prey on the vulnerability of young models, who are often foreign, lonely and not working very much. By

---

[45] Jennifer Sky, 'Young models are easy pickings for the city's club promoters', *Observer*, 22 September 2014. https://observer.com/2014/09/young-models-are-easy-pickings-for-the-citys-club-promoters/

filling exclusive clubs with beautiful girls, people may be more encouraged to spend thousands of pounds on alcohol in order to sexually exploit them. I know many models who have been spiked with drugs in clubs and have been spiked myself in the past, which leads to terrible situations. This further extends to taking models on 'holidays' where they may be offered huge sums of money to have sex with people or find themselves in extreme danger.

Club promoters may seem extremely nice and can groom models by becoming their friends or starting a relationship of debt where the model feels obliged. I believe that there are even apps run by club promoters that appear to offer something completely different, such as free gifts, as a way to lure models in.

Many exclusive clubs hire promoters to bring models out, especially on weekdays when most people are at work! On any day of the week, models can go for free dinner and as much free alcohol as they can handle at the top clubs in a city. Tables at these clubs are often sold for over £1000 each, with alcohol around the same price – I have seen people pay £30,000 bills for one night.

In particular, these clubs may appeal to incredibly rich, older men who want access to models. By ordering metre-long bottles of vodka, complete with sparklers and half-naked women, they are demonstrating how rich they are. So they flock to the places with the most models who are willing to sleep with them, which the clubs capitalise on. As a model out with a promoter, I would always have a full glass of vodka in my hand and have been offered free drugs several times. The promoters may have their own table and then filter models off to other tables, selling them without their knowledge. Sadly, I know models who have been raped due to these situations.

Models may also be invited out for free dinners by club promoters as a way of encouraging them to go clubbing afterwards. In some cases, the promoters may be paid by private clients for models to attend these dinners, who have absolutely no idea of what is happening. These are very dangerous as models can be exposed to very untrustworthy, powerful people. I know a model who was offered £20,000 in cash for sex.

Promoters may also invite models to free events and holidays without realising they are being paid for their attendance – even though many may seem very legitimate, such as club openings or film festivals. These may often be part of a bigger plot where the models will be 'looked after' by a certain person and required to attend other events such as dinners as a result, potentially leading to prostitution.[46]

These dinners and holidays can place models in a bizarre alternate reality where they cannot afford to buy themselves food from a supermarket but can dine at the top restaurants in the city. They are not working at all but are being called beautiful by celebrities and millionaires. They can't pay their rent but are mingling in mansions and scenes where thousands of pounds pass hands as easily as cigarettes. With no friends or support in their daily lives, they have people that seemingly do not want anything from them other than to feed them and introduce them to nice, successful people – it is a hard thing for adults to get their head around, let alone a drunk teenager actually in that situation!

The reality is that many models may end up severely sexually assaulted and as prostitutes, because they become addicted to the glamour and money and cannot face their real lives – a distorted sense of reality that fuels deep depression, as seen in 'Z is for Zen'. Although escorting typically happens to females, there is also the potential for male models to be escorts too, paid by women and men for their presence, which is very emasculating and can lead to the same slippery slope. It is a world that fuels drug and alcohol addiction and is extremely dangerous.

---

46 Clare Conway interviewing Jazz Egger, 'How it feels to... expose the seedy side of modelling. By the catwalk model Jazz Egger', *The Sunday Times*, 10 December 2017; 'asking if I'd like to go on a yacht to Greece with three millionaires. I said: "Why would anyone pay me to go on holiday?"'

By being aware of these practices, models can protect themselves. Exploitative practices by a promoter aren't limited to, but may include:

- Scouting models on the street and asking for their personal details.
- Harassing models by excessive communication.
- Inviting models out for lunch or dinner, or to events, clubs and parties; if they aren't friends with you, there is no reason for you to attend.
- Giving models gifts or free experiences such as lunches and clothes.
- Posing as a legitimate business such as an events company or app, and inviting models out to situations where they are given alcohol/drugs.
- Convincing models to hide things from their agencies by telling them to book out days to attend holidays or providing them with secret paid work.
- Giving or spiking models with drugs/alcohol.
- Telling models they can't leave a situation and creating a feeling of obligation; this may be done by providing transport home at the end of the night.
- Introducing models to exploitative private clients or people.
- Falsely claiming to be affiliated with agencies.
- Sexually abusing a model or making them feel uncomfortable.
- Receiving money on behalf of models from clients and clubs.
- Inviting models on holidays and to events where they will be exploited.
- Offering models money for attendance or sexual favours.

Sexual exploitation by those in powerful positions

Models regularly interact with people in incredibly powerful positions – everyone from royalty to the owners of companies. They may be very easily manipulated by these people, being offered seemingly legitimate routes out of modelling and an 'easy ride'. I have been offered numerous jobs by rich, older men who have not even looked at my CV, where every situation turned out to be potentially sexually exploitative.

There is a difference between empowered networking (as seen in 'N is for Networking') and manipulation. If something sounds too good to be true, it probably is. Nothing is for free, especially when there is beauty involved.

Sexually exploitative practices by powerful people are not limited to, but can include:

- Meeting with a model on an unprofessional basis or contacting them outside of work with the intention of 'getting to know them' in an inappropriate way, such as texting late at night.
- Offering a model a job who is completely inexperienced and not suitable for the job, especially with high salaries involved.
- Organising an interview that is not professional, for example, at a restaurant, hotel or the private home of the person.
- Offering very high salaries that seem too good to be true.
- Making sexual advances/sexually abusing a model.
- Humiliating a model who is working for them by making sexual or offensive jokes and comments.
- Offering a model any drugs or alcohol.
- Buying gifts for a model that they cannot repay.
- Offering a model to go on any kind of trip with them.
- Offering a job based on something else, such as going on a date.
- Offering a model an informal job with no salary, often masked as an internship.

Models must be empowered enough to be able to recognise sexually exploitative situations and avoid them altogether. If you happen to find yourself in one, do not hesitate to leave immediately. Nothing is more important than your safety. Models must have these foundations of self-confidence and personal safety as basic starting blocks for being self-employed, before being able to move onto more complex areas such as tax, which we will see in the next chapter.

Anti-exploitation tips

- Become a member of the models' union Equity, which provides independent advice and legal support, as seen in 'U is for Unionising'. Always refer anything you do not feel comfortable with to them.
- Recognise when you are being treated inappropriately and speak out – all that is needed is, 'you are making me feel uncomfortable'.
- Always have a chaperone with you whenever possible, especially if a job involves being alone with one other person or if you are under the age of 18.
- Ensure that anyone who wants to touch you obtains your express permission first.
- Know that you can always say no to anything and will always be supported by your agency.
- Take self-defence classes and carry a rape alarm – it is a good idea to have one on your keyring.
- Always have a portable and wall phone charger with you.
- Know your boundaries and what you feel comfortable with, and relay this to your agency.
- Have a respectful relationship of honest communication with your bookers, including having procedures such as calling the agency with a 'safe word' you can say on the telephone in case of dangerous situations arising.
- Never engage in unprofessional, especially sexual behaviour with anyone related to work such as a booker or photographer. Avoid any events with these people that are not strictly professional.
- Refer any private communications by someone related to work to your bookers or Equity. Ignore and block all people who harass you or make you feel uncomfortable.
- Undertake a risk assessment when meeting new people and on jobs, assessing the potential risks and exits should danger

occur. Look out for hidden cameras, especially in private locations such as bedrooms.

- Double-check all addresses and names of clients online and never enter into a situation that doesn't feel right.
- Never accept drugs, cigarettes or alcohol, especially in professional situations.
- Only travel abroad for work if you feel 100% comfortable in doing so.
- Never lose control of your passport, especially while abroad.
- Ask your agency to line up castings/test shoots with another model so you are not alone. Also ask your agency to ensure no shoots are ever located in a photographer's house.
- Never undress in front of anyone without feeling 100% comfortable to do so and having the option of a private changing room.
- Call the police in any emergency.
- Prioritise your health and wellbeing in any situation, thinking about the broader consequences on your life.
- Always have a back-up plan and write any important information such as contact numbers and addresses down on paper, especially when travelling.
- Never go out with a promoter in any capacity – for lunch, dinner or drinks.
- Be street-smart, for example, avoid careless phone use in public and wear mirrored sunglasses to avoid eye contact with predators. See more in 'D is for Danger'.
- Never accept gifts from anyone you do not know personally and always remember that nothing is for free.
- Be very cautious of offers of help by people you work with. Avoid spending any time alone with them that is outside of working hours.
- Never, ever accept offers of money, regardless of the situation. There is no such thing as free money. It is always better to ask for help from friends and family rather than anyone professionally related.

- Avoid jobs that do not seem legitimate, such as a trip abroad where a model will be paid to just 'have fun'. If it seems too good to be true, it probably is, even if it is proposed by your agency.
- Have a strong support system that checks in on a daily basis with you, such as family chat groups.
- Be very cautious of job offers, especially ones with unusually high or low salaries and where the interview process is unprofessional.

is for Tax

IF I HAD a pound for every model who thinks they don't have to pay tax, I would have enough to pay my tax bill!

Models have lots of misconceptions about tax, such as not having to pay tax or being able to claim for anything related to modelling at all, such as gym memberships, as tax-deductible expenses. This is mainly due to models starting as teenagers, the global nature of the job and the fact that no one sits down and tells models exactly what they need to know.

Paying tax in the UK as a self-employed model is actually fairly simple once you understand the basics. In this chapter, I will explain this and show you how to protect yourself from legal issues in the future by keeping on top of your tax in the most legal and efficient way. Remember that this advice is formed of my own opinion and should not be relied upon – it is always advisable to use an industry-specialised accountant when it comes to specific tax returns.

Did you know?

1. Models are self-employed, so their agencies and clients do not pay any of a model's tax in the UK – models must declare this to HMRC each year and pay it out of their own income.

2. Models have to declare their income even if they haven't made enough to pay any tax.

3. You will need to show tax statements for things such as buying a house, so it is important to stay organised with your returns.

4. When models go years without paying tax, they have to backtrack and pay tax for those years missed – possibly encountering fines.

Should you get an accountant?

The majority of models won't necessarily need an accountant to file their returns – it is very simple to register online with HRMC, list your income and expenses at the end of the year and they will calculate your tax. However, an industry-specialised accountant can be extremely helpful in ensuring your tax return is most efficient and correct, especially if you earn a high income (over £80,000) or work abroad. Working abroad comes with many complications due to local government laws which will be different to the UK.

It is important to use an accountant with specific knowledge of the modelling industry as it is so unique – the best one for models in London is widely acknowledged to be GBP Associates.[47]

I advise using an accountant if you are earning a relatively high income, work abroad, have an issue with your tax such as missed financial years or simply want to find out how you can save more

---

[47] GBP Associates. http://www.gbpassociates.com/

on tax payments. It is incredibly helpful to use an accountant but not strictly necessary.

How to manage your taxes as a UK model

This may change in the upcoming years with different political and technological developments, but for now, at least, this is how to master the basics for a model.

1. Register as self-employed and prepare yourself.

    Do this very quick, easy process as soon as you start modelling by registering with HRMC online.[48] You have to do this by 5 October after the end of the tax year during which you became self-employed, but it is easy to do it straight away so you don't forget.

    Self-employed models will pay tax on the profit they make with their business expenses deducted from their overall income. Currently, If your taxable income is under £40,000, you will be paying roughly 20% of your income over the personal allowance in tax. If you earn over £40,000, you will be paying 35–45% on the excess amount above this. This can be estimated online during the year if a model has relatively predictable income (highly doubtful!). It is worked out after the financial year is over, so it is important that models save enough to pay their tax as they have no guarantee of future work!

    Tips
    o   Register as self-employed as soon as you can.
    o   Set up a savings account to automatically divert 30% of your income.
    o   Set up a debit account purely for income and expenses related to modelling.

---

[48] UK Government, 'Register for and file your Self Assessment tax return'. www.gov.uk/log-in-file-self-assessment-tax-return

2. File your self-assessment tax return on time.

To do this, you will need to know the below information and fill in the paper or online form.

o Financial year: the year your income is assessed from and to. At the time of writing the UK financial year is generally 6 April–5 April.

o Deadline: at the time of writing, the deadline to submit a paper tax return for the previous financial year is the end of October, and for filing online is the end of January, with tax payable also at the end of January. You can pay quarterly or in one lump sum.

Tips

o File your tax return as early as you can so it is out of the way – around October.

o Make sure you don't miss any dates, or you can be fined and charged interest.

3. Work out your resident status and taxable income.

o Resident status: the country where you will pay tax as a resident. If you are a UK tax resident, you will pay tax on your worldwide income. If you live and work in the UK then you will be a UK tax resident; working internationally causes this to become complicated. As soon as you start spending more time abroad it is always advisable to use an accountant.

o Taxable income: the money received during the financial year, less tax-deductible expenses. You can ask your agency accountant(s) for a full financial statement for the last year to see this. Taxable income covers any money you made during that year. If you are employed by another job you may have already had that tax automatically deducted (in a process called PAYE, 'pay as you earn'), which you will list on the return.

o Personal income allowance: a tax-free allowance for UK residents on their overall income. It changes yearly and depending on overall income, but at the time of writing it would be around £11,000–12,000 for most people. If you haven't earned over this allowance, you won't be paying any tax!

Tips

o If you are often travelling for work, make sure you keep note of how many days you are in the UK and other countries (to assist with assessing your resident status).

o Remember that you will have to file a tax return if you earn any money in the UK, even if you aren't a tax resident.

o Don't forget to include all money received commercially, such as property revenue and bank interest.

4. Work out your expenses.

o Tax-deductible expenses: you can deduct business expenses from your overall income to find the profit made, allowing you to lower the income that you will pay tax on. If this falls below the personal allowance, a model will not pay tax that year.

o Business expenses: these are costs wholly and exclusively incurred in the performance of the business. The duality-of-purpose test[49] states that if an expense could be used for a non-business purpose as well as a business purpose, it will usually not qualify as a tax-deductible expense. This means expenses must only be used for your business – decide whether you would be spending that money if you were not a model, and if you can prove this. This is fairly easy for things such as taxis to jobs but not so easy for expenses such as clothes; how can you prove that you wouldn't buy that t-shirt if you weren't a model? Proof can be obtained by paperwork (physical or virtual), including receipts, emails and financial and bank statements. Here

---

[49] HMRC, Business Income Manual. www.gov.uk/hmrc-internal-manuals/business-income-manual/bim37600

are examples of what can theoretically be claimed as business expenses if they satisfy the requirements.

◊ Union fees, if the organisation is approved by HMRC.

◊ Some expenses that you were instructed to pay for/ were advanced/charged for by your agency, such as specific hair appointments for a casting/job, test shoots, marketing fees.

◊ Food and drink. When travel costs have been incurred for work, it is allowed to claim reasonable expenses on food and drink, usually under £10 per day. This may include purchases on casting days.

◊ Hotel-related expenses. For example, accommodation fees if you have to stay in a hotel for a specific job/ casting. Sundry (excessive) expenses such as the minibar and newspapers are not claimable.

◊ Travel to and from castings/jobs, such as public transport, flights, mileage claim and taxis.

◊ Car-related expenses. If you use your personal car, then you can claim 45p per mile for business mileage for the first 10,000 miles (25p thereafter).

◊ Computers and software related to modelling. Software such as Microsoft office, Adobe, Portfolio Apps, Dropbox, Photoshop and website subscription/hosting fees.

◊ Stationery and mailing expenses.

◊ Working from home. Models could claim certain expenses by using their home as their office if they manage their work from there. HMRC have a weekly allowance.

◊ Accountancy fees.

◊ Phone and internet costs.

Tips

o ALWAYS make sure you list these expenses if you have earned over the personal allowance – I didn't do it at first because it was all too confusing and complicated!

o   Ask your agency to put into writing or give you all receipts related to any money they ask you to spend. Remember that not everything they tell you to buy, or say is claimable as an expense, can actually be claimed.

o   Use a separate debit card for all of your business-related income and expenses.

o   Note all of the dates of your work (including castings) on a spreadsheet alongside the expenses. HMRC could ask where you went in that taxi and for proof of the casting/job.

o   Get in the habit of photographing all of your receipts and uploading them to a virtual folder. Remember that your bank account is a good way of tracking expenses, but HMRC may require the receipt as proof if you are investigated.

o   Remember to keep your expenses reasonable – dramatic expenses will rarely be allowed – but do not be afraid to spend money in the course of your business as a model!

5.   Pay your tax and National Insurance.

When you receive your tax bill, pay it as soon as possible. Your tax return will show you how much and when to pay, including your income tax and National Insurance contributions for that year. HMRC will also send reminders.

If you have already filed a tax return previously, you may already have paid tax by 'payment on account'. This is when HMRC charge two instalments per year by estimating your future tax off your previous one, spreading out the cost of the year's tax. You have to do this if your tax is over £1000. Helpful for those with a steady income – not so helpful for those who can't predict their income at all!

By taking responsibility for your own tax, you can protect yourself against people who may be able to use this lack of knowledge against you. Ensure that your return is paid on time every year and have a firm handle on your accounts. Being self-employed opens you up to enormous vulnerabilities if you don't understand what it involves, which is where unions come in handy. In the past models have not enjoyed the protection of traditional employment unions as self-employed workers; however, there are several different ways around this that we will see in the next chapter.

is for Unionizing

ONE OF THE biggest reasons that models are exploited is because they lack any real protection – from the government, agencies or clients. Everyone has an ulterior motive (usually profit) and models themselves have such short, divided and competitive careers that they find it difficult enough to make friends with each other, let alone come together to form a united union.

In the UK, there is a lack of official unions for self-employed workers. This is ironic when these are usually the people who need them the most – for whom work is in such short supply that they are open to exploitation as a result, often not being paid at all or for months after a job. As modelling is such a fragmented, global job it is difficult for models to effectively unionise themselves, and this will continue until they are finally empowered to stand up for themselves and other models.

Unions are societies of people with a common interest, traditionally formed to enjoy bargaining power as a collective. In this chapter, I will identify the trade union partly representing the interests of models and question why models have not been afforded proper protection by unions previously, which involves looking at the employment status of models in reality. Importantly, I will also demonstrate how you can start unionising yourself along with your fellow models, which is an incredibly liberating and empowering thing to do.

Did you know?

1. Equity[50] is a trade union partly representing UK-based models; however, very few models understand what Equity can do for them or even know about its existence.

2. Being a part of a trade union can offer you independent advice, support and perks such as insurance.

3. Models can make a real change in their own careers by speaking out and using their voice.

Current trade unions for models

A trade union is a membership-based organisation representing workers in a certain industry, with the aim of protecting and advancing their interests.

To become an actor in the UK, it is usually necessary to register with Equity first as a requirement of joining an acting agency. Equity is a union representing those in the entertainment industry, including models as of 2009. Contrastingly, most models have rarely heard of Equity and may even be encouraged not to join, scared of feedback from their agencies. It is hard for Equity to represent models' interests if they don't represent them!

For a nominal membership fee, Equity model members receive legal support, including legal action to recover payment, free tax

---

[50] Equity Models Network. www.equity.org.uk/getting-involved/networks/models-network/

advice and insurance (£10 million public liability insurance and accident insurance, especially in case of facial disfigurement; see 'D is for Dangers'). They are becoming well-respected in the industry, working with the British Fashion Council[51] and the British Fashion Model Agents Association[52] for models. However, Equity have limited power, which is dependent on them being acknowledged by the industry and their work actually being enforced. The union itself is also not organised by models and at the time of writing, there are no active meetings for models being held.

Other recognised unions for models around the world as of 2019 include Model Union Denmark[53] (DaMo) and the Model Alliance[54] in the USA, founded by model Sara Ziff. The Model Alliance has launched several influential campaigns, including its RESPECT Program, which is a legally binding agreement to protect models from sexual harassment and abuse, an enforceable code for the fashion industry with consequences if it is broken. The Model Alliance is very active in campaigning for changes in US law to protect models and have undertaken several influential model surveys referenced in this book.

Ultimately, as modelling is such a global job, with many models not based in any one country, a global-reaching union is needed, formed of models themselves. They are truly the only people who can understand the unique problems that face their industry.

Self-employment test

Models remain largely legally unprotected by the government by virtue of their status as self-employed workers,[55] which is why

---

[51] http://www.britishfashioncouncil.com/

[52] https://bfma.fashion

[53] http://danskemodeller.dk/

[54] http://modelalliance.org/

[55] UK Government, 'Working for yourself'. www.gov.uk/working-for-yourself

some form of unionising is required. The test of self-employment in the UK involves the following.

1. Control: who holds control over task, mode, means and timing of work?

   As model agencies contractually require models to attend any jobs they book for them and organise their work completely, including signing them into foreign contracts, it is clear that models do not have any control over their work beyond choosing which mother agency to join. Models have a duty to obey their agency's orders (especially in terms of how they look and who they work for), do not choose their hours of work past booking out certain days with prior permission and are supervised at work due to reports being made to their agency. Typically most model agency contracts are exclusive, meaning models can only have one agency per territory and usually one global mother agency worldwide to manage these subsidiary agencies for a model.

2. Integration: how integral is a model's work to the business?

   Models are the focus of their agencies, who lock them into contracts they cannot leave without extensive notice periods. Jobs they are booked on cannot be performed without the model and they themselves cannot be replaced by another model, as they will not have the same exact features. Different models can command different rates of pay.

3. Economic reality: where does the financial risk lie?

   Models rely completely on their agencies to be paid, are not usually able to work with other agencies or clients without telling their agency and experiencing a real loss in work or breaking a contract, cannot provide replacements if they don't want to do a job and are rarely allowed to cancel a booked job in case of sickness. Their agencies have the power of attorney to book them onto whatever work they like without permission and models encounter any financial risk themselves as most contracts hold the model financially responsible. Models invest in their own business as a result of their agency's instructions, often having money spent in their name without even being told!

Models pay tax via self-assessment but most have no idea that they should do this, so many do not. They are not paid for holidays or sick days because they don't have any at all! Models are expected to be ready to work at all times, regardless of what day of the week it is or notice given unless they have 'booked off' in advance, giving a reason why. This booking-off usually amounts to the least amount possible, such as an hour for lunch with friends, and booking entire days off is frowned upon. Even weekends have to be booked off. Booked-off periods are rarely actually valid holidays because a model's agency will still contact them (even if it is to send their schedule for the next day) and pressure them to take jobs if they come up.

4. Mutuality of obligation: is there an equal relationship?

I don't think it is possible to look at a model and say they have an equal relationship to their agency. Their employment periods are incredibly short, their contracts are entirely one-sided and they may or may not work. Some contracts can tie them to an agency for years, where they are not allowed to work outside of the agency, but the agency doesn't have to get them any work! They are not realistically allowed to refuse any work as they will be punished for this.

The UK government needs to reassess the employment status of models so that they can be afforded the protection they deserve. They are much more vulnerable, young and exploited than most employees, without any real control over their careers.

Models can raise awareness about the realities of the industry to help others understand their often-hidden issues and bring about real, lasting change that can positively impact members of society overall, who will hopefully stop comparing themselves to models!

How models can unionise themselves

You don't need to be part of the government to bring about change. It is incredibly empowering to take it on yourself and use your voice to talk about issues that affect you. Models don't have to accept the terrible working conditions they face every day – by coming together as one and speaking out about abusive practices, asking for protection and showing why it is so important, they can quite literally change their own industry. Examples of how easy this is can already be seen by media campaigns such as #MeToo[56] and #Myjobshouldnotincludeabuse.[57] Just after Charli Howard[58] spoke out about the pressure from her agency to lose weight, she was signed in New York and is a very successful model today. When Rosalie Nelson[59] formed a petition against forcing models to be unhealthy, she obtained over 100,000 signatures and was heard by the government as a result.

You should not be punished for speaking out honestly, and if you are then it is a sign you're with the wrong agency! Fighting for a better workplace is empowering and provides a huge opportunity to make the world a better place.

You can follow @themodelmanifesto on Instagram and go to www.themodelmanifesto.com to find out how you can be involved in unionising models in the UK.

---

[56] Louise Burke, 'The #MeToo shockwave: how the movement has reverberated around the world', *The Telegraph*, 9 March 2018. www.telegraph.co.uk/news/world/metoo-shockwave/

[57] Emilia Petrarca, 'The fashion industry starts its own harassment hashtag, *The Cut*, 13 December 2018. www.thecut.com/2017/10/fashion-industry-harassment-cameron-russell-instagram.html

[58] Eva Wiseman, 'Model Charli Howard: "They told me I was fat"', *Guardian*, 28 January 2018. www.theguardian.com/lifeandstyle/2018/jan/28/model-charli-howard-fashion-body-positive-they-told-me-i-was-fat

[59] Change.org, 'Create a law to protect models from getting dangerously skinny!' www.change.org/p/jackiedp-help-protect-models-from-getting-dangerously-skinny-rosalienelson-modelslaw-lfw

Examples of how you as a model can unionise yourself and raise awareness include the following.

- Joining a union for models, or starting one yourself! Telling everyone you know about the union, especially other models.
- Speaking out about the industry honestly and impartially. Don't blame people, lie or exaggerate – the truth is often shocking enough. It is generally advisable not to name certain companies or people because this can spark off a legal battle. It's usually clear enough for people to work out themselves. This is good to do in person and via social media, especially Instagram.
- Addressing practical issues that are really affecting models, such as financial exploitation, in a mature way instead of moaning, for example by complaining about the lack of work.
- Starting a blog to highlight the injustices in the industry. Rebecca Pearson created a great blog to help models, modeltypeface.com, which has led to a career in journalism.
- Starting a podcast or YouTube channel with other models.
- Writing a column for a magazine or newspaper about modelling. I have regularly written on models' rights for a magazine, which has been a great way to keep up with changes in the industry.
- Lobbying your local MP about models' issues.
- Writing and proposing changes to your agency or union to implement.
- Organising regular meetings for models to discuss the issues in the industry and what can be done. Sharing information with each other about abusive practices and people so you can protect yourselves.
- Thinking of social media campaigns that can spread across the world, such as highlighting the lack of racial diversity in the modelling industry. Things that affect general society are great because people can identify with your campaign. Hashtags and buzzwords such as feminism are good to start spreading these. Facebook is great for your post being shared

virally and Instagram is excellent to start a movement where people share their own experiences.

- Lobbying the press and speaking about your issues to journalists and news reporters.
- Holding events and peaceful demonstrations to raise awareness, such as a debate with models.
- Starting petitions about the issues you care about.
- Creating a documentary or art show, for example, a photoshoot, showing the different ways a model can be exploited.
- Collaborating with other companies, charities and industry players such as your agency. It is good to be respectful at all times and give people the opportunity to explain why things are the way they are and how they can be changed so you can work together. Teamwork is key to creating real, lasting change.
- Supporting your fellow models and ensuring they are heard.
- Writing a book like this one!

One voice is not as effective as a hundred or a thousand. The power of unionising is evident – by using your voice you are able to empower others and make a real change. Models globally need to form together to protect themselves and future models from suffering the exploitation exposed in this book as a routine part of the job. As we will see in the next chapter, there is a myriad of ways that models can be abused, where their safety, wellbeing and interests are simply ignored in favour of making profit for somebody else.

The time has never been better to stand up for those who need it, starting with yourself.

is for Visas

Oबtaining a visa to work in a country can be one of the most important yet forgotten details of modelling. When a model signs with a new international agency it is very exciting, and often the last thing on their mind is whether they are actually able to legally work in that country. It is the responsibility of the model, not the agent, to sort the visa. While the majority of agencies help obtain their models legitimate visas, some agencies may know how to avoid the law as it is quicker and cheaper and may encourage this.

Models are often encouraged to work illegally, without a proper working visa, in order to make those around them money, quickly. Visa processes can be long and difficult, and the instantaneous, global nature of modelling does not always work with this. In this chapter, I will explain how models can be manipulated in terms of working visas and how they can best protect themselves against this by ensuring they always have the legal right to work.

Did you know?

1. Models are often encouraged to work illegally without a valid working visa.

2. It is the responsibility of the model to have a proper working visa and they can be arrested as a result of working illegally.[60]

3. If a model doesn't have a valid visa to work in a country, they have no proper legal entitlement to be paid!

When and why do models need working visas?

There is a lot of confusion about what amounts to work requiring a visa for models, but it is better to always be safe and assume that any paid work requires a visa. The cost of getting this wrong can result in you being banned from a country, or even imprisonment.

Work abroad can mean shoots abroad with whole teams flying out, direct bookings of models to other countries or models going to live in a new country for a few months 'on stay'. More on this can be seen in 'O is for Overseas'.

Immigration authorities are very used to models entering the country under the guise of a holiday when they are actually working. Very well-known agencies may assure a model that it is fine to visit under a tourist visa and do a few jobs here and there, as some have done to me. This is illegal and you are the only one who will suffer the consequences – you have no real entitlement to be paid for your work and can have the rest of your life affected as a result. Agencies do not have the power to circumvent the law and immigration authorities.

---

[60] Linda Sharkey, 'Over 60 models arrested in Beijing for working illegally', *The Independent*, 13 May 2014. www.independent.co.uk/life-style/fashion/news/over-60-models-arrested-in-beijing-for-working-illegally-9364739.html

It is also very dangerous for you to work abroad as a model in this way, as you are in an incredibly vulnerable position. First, you do not speak the language and are often alone, so it is much harder to understand your job and communicate with your agency. Second, modelling can be very different in different countries, and you can easily be blackmailed into doing things you don't feel comfortable with as a result of your illegal working status. This can even end up in sex trafficking and human slavery. Someone once attempted to kidnap me while working abroad! Many models are targeted by club promoters who prey on their vulnerability while travelling alone, as seen in 'S is for Sexual Exploitation'.

Finally, models who work illegally have no legal right to be paid for any work, even if there is a contract in place. Without a working visa, they will have voided the contract by working illegally. In the majority of contracts, it will explicitly state that models are entirely responsible for their visas, so it doesn't make a difference to an agency if a model is arrested or not. On the contrary, if they are working illegally it will mean that the agency can technically keep any money they make!

It is hard enough already to be paid by foreign agencies, let alone ones who can legally keep your money. There are stories of some agencies paying models in cash, who were sent through customs with their shoes stuffed with banknotes – trafficking money. This is completely illegal and often also means that the model is being hugely underpaid as there are no proper, transparent invoices. Not to mention, being paid in cash becomes very difficult when declaring your income for tax purposes. More can be seen in 'T is for Tax'.

In the UK, model agencies have to sponsor foreign models who wish to work here and need a licence to do so.[61] It is important for models to remember that once they have a visa that is sponsored by a particular agency, that agency technically owns them and

---

[61] UK Government, 'Temporary Worker – Government Authorised Exchange visa (Tier 5)'. www.gov.uk/tier-5-government-authorised-exchange

they will not be able to change without undergoing the entire, expensive process again. This may result in many damaging situations where models are terribly exploited by the agency sponsoring them, which exerts a huge amount of power as they are unable to work elsewhere.

I have had agencies that made vague assurances of visas only to arrive and discover they haven't obtained me a proper visa and wanted to pay me by cash, with the visa taking up to two months to obtain and requiring me to leave the country first on a 'visa run'. I left immediately but had already paid for my flights and rent – it is not always so easy for a model to leave a country once they have spent this money! Despite this, it is vitally important that they leave immediately if they do not have a working visa or there is anything dodgy – their entire safety is at risk and it is always worth the money to get out of such situations as quickly as possible.

Each country requires a model to have a different visa in order to be able to work there. A model agency will always know the legal visa requirements for working in that country and if they are avoiding them, this should be a big red flag! Models should ask to see their working visa for every single job that they are requested to do abroad, and remember the importance of their safety over potentially huge sums of money. I know of several models who flew to America for a huge campaign only to be arrested at the airport and deported, meaning they were banned from the country for several years. Obviously they weren't paid, and they could even technically have been sued by the client for not turning up to the job! If anyone is ever trying to tell you that you don't need a visa, they are wrong.

How do models get working visas?

Every country will have a different visa policy, usually relating to the nationality of the model. Therefore, visas are done on a case-by-case basis, but generally a model agency based in the country of work will be able to help guide a model through the visa process. You may need to engage a lawyer, but usually good agencies should help models through these processes and give specific advice and help relevant to the model.

It is therefore very important to trust the foreign agency, which can be hard if you have never met them before! Some agencies may add on hidden fees for these visa costs (as seen in 'E is for Expenses'), whereas others may give you incorrect advice, so it is important to always trust your own gut instinct and research the visa requirements for a particular country yourself, online. Your agency can then act as a guide.

The US visa[62] for models is notoriously one of the hardest visas to secure, as it usually involves a high fee, a long waiting period and models to demonstrate they have 'special talent'. Other places, such as Australia, may offer models the opportunity to work for a period of time as part of their Working Holiday Scheme. With all of the changes taking place on the international playing field this will only become more segregated, so it is important for models to do their own research and decide which countries to go to based on that.

As we will see in the next chapter, visas are particularly important when models are travelling around in quick succession, for example, during 'Fashion Week', where some models may be expected to work in four countries in one month.

Anti-exploitation tips

- Always ask your agency to tell you about any visa requirements, remembering to double-check this before confirming any jobs shooting abroad.
- Read all of your foreign contracts properly, having a lawyer check over them.

---

[62] 'Visa requirements for models', *The Fashion Law*, 17 September 2016. www.thefashionlaw.com/learn/models-visa-requirements

- Go on holiday to the country you'd like to work in first, ensuring you like the agency you are signed by. Remember, your visa may be tied to them.
- Research the visas online and speak to various agencies about what visa is best.
- Remember to ask around about your visa costs. In America, there are various types of visas and hugely varying fees – one agency wanted to charge me £3000 yet with another I paid £1500. These may include lawyers' costs, and be overpriced. The agency may also advance part of the cost of the visa, so you should check with them the total cost.
- Understand how complicated visa processes can be – for the USA you may need to provide several letters of recommendation from industry professionals and show you are established in your field. Processing times can take several months and this is why agencies often prefer to avoid this.
- Avoid allowing your agency to expense your visa for you, as it will mean you are in debt before even arriving in the country.
- Always have a copy of your visa to fly with.
- Remember that visas may not apply to the entire country. For example, in the USA visas may be dependent on states or particular branches of an agency. Always check this with your agency and be clear about where you can and can't work.
- Make sure you actually want to go to that country for work – it is pretty pointless buying a visa if you don't want to work there! Weigh up the costs and benefits and make your own decision.
- Don't be convinced into going to a country for 'castings' under a holiday visa, as you will just be spending money and likely getting into debt to your agency! You will have to have a working visa to do the jobs, so it's pretty pointless going for castings.
- Never, ever work without a proper visa. If you find yourself in such a situation, get out of it as soon as possible.

is for Walk

A MODEL'S 'WALK' is their unique way of walking down the runway. It embodies their essence and is something uniquely undefinable, which is why many models desperately spend a lot of money and time trying to achieve a strong walk. Fashion shows can be very exploitative of models, especially during 'Fashion Week', so in this chapter I will show how models can walk away from anything that does not serve them.

Did you know?

1. Not all models can be runway models. See the different types of work for models in 'J is for Jobs'.

2. Runway models are generally required to be over 5'11" tall (male and female) and very thin.

3. There is an intense amount of lead-up to Fashion Week shows, including sessions where the clothes are made on the models, called fittings.

4. Models will attend 15 to 30 castings per day in the days before Fashion Week shows.

What is a model's walk?

Runway models will often be asked to show their walk to people – usually their agency or a casting director. This involves walking up and down a room, with a pose at the end of the imaginary catwalk. The walk must be strong, confident and demand all of the attention in the room.

Sounds simple, right? Unfortunately, a model's walk is something they spend years trying to perfect. When I started modelling, I had to go to a model school to walk up and down a mirrored room for hours every Saturday, paying £80 each time! Models suffer with their walk due to a lack of confidence or lack of awareness in their own body, sometimes with a strange quirk such as one arm swinging wildly or hunched shoulders. They may look a bit scared or try and cross their legs to look like the models they have seen on television.

There is also the small issue of high heels. Finding the right high heels makes the world of difference to your walk – I used to try and walk in my eight-inch stilettos and looked like a baby giraffe failing at exuding confidence. Nowadays, I have shoes that I know make me look and feel good and I know will enable me to walk confidently. The client isn't looking at the size of your heels – they are looking at your facial expression and your body.

For models there may be several dangers accompanied with walking shows, as seen in 'D is for Dangers'. It may be difficult to walk in the heels, to guess when the end of the runway is, to not look down and check your legs are still there or to avoid the criticising gaze of strangers watching you walk. All of these worries show in the way that you walk.

Therefore, the best advice I can give on perfecting your catwalk is improving your own self-confidence. The biggest realisation I had was that I could just walk normally – there was no special way I had to walk, no particular way of holding my shoulders or crossing my feet, I could just walk as though I would down the street and this is enough, because I look confident in myself. I know how to walk down the street!

Good methods of improving your confidence are identified in 'Z is for Zen'; however, other ways could include walking in front of a mirror or somebody you trust at home and filming your walk. Watch it back and spot anything you may do when you are nervous so you can work on being mindful about these quirks. Watch if you walk too quickly or too slowly and the expression on your face. I always fix my eyes on a spot at the back of the room and breathe out of my mouth, clearing my mind as I walk down a runway. This helps me forget that anybody else is in the room.

You should never be pressured to pay anyone to teach you how to walk, as I was. No one can truly teach this or tell you when you are 'ready', as it all comes from within and finding your own confidence.

How are runway models exploited?

Runway models' careers tend to centre around Fashion Week. This is the presentation of a country's top designers' new collections, so most countries have their own Fashion Week. The most important ones are accepted as being New York, Paris, Milan and London, which take place over one month – September/February for female models and January/June for male models, generally speaking. Models are expected to be in peak physical condition because there is so much competition, which sadly often equates to being as thin as possible, resulting in immense, unhealthy pressure.

Fashion Week can be extremely exploitative. First, the castings take place a few days before the shows, due to the models travelling from country to country – often without valid working visas, as seen in 'V is for Visas'. They are likely only in the country for one week, so it is highly dubious that models would undergo long visa processes for this, leaving them open to breaking the law and the potential to be arrested, and other extreme exploitation such as not being paid at all. Models are often staying in model apartments, as seen in 'O is for Overseas', which are often extortionately priced and very bad quality.

The castings themselves can be very exploitative, with models queuing for hours to be seen for seconds, herded around and visiting up to 40 clients per day. There is one particularly degrading casting in London where around 20 clients sit in a room as models walk from table to table, handing composite cards over and showing their walk. It is quite literally like being in a market of rather beautiful cattle. Cards are usually disposed on the 'no' pile and models are rejected to their face, as up to 1000 models visit this casting in a day.

Other castings can be exploitative as models are treated much worse than their usual castings due to the sheer volume of models – they may be made to wait for hours and rejected much more brutally. Models are also often charged extra to be a part of 'Fashion Week packages' by their agency, usually involving extra composite cards being printed for castings.

It is a very physically and mentally exhausting time for models. If they are optioned for any shows, they may attend fittings where the clothes are tried on them prior to the show. These fittings have traditionally been unpaid and can go on for many hours into the early morning, with models unable to leave and all undressing in a room of naked models.

If they are confirmed for the booking after all of this, then they may have a few shows per day. Fashion Week tends to have 'on-schedule' shows, which are the very famous designers who have supermodels flaunting their designs down the famous Fashion Week runways, and 'off-schedule' shows, which are essentially every single designer who wants to hop onto the Fashion Week bandwagon. These designers are much more exploitative of models as they are far less regulated and may be from overseas, having travelled to a location specifically for the shows, being unaware of how models are generally treated in other countries.

Fashion shows are notoriously badly paid, whether on- or off-schedule. I have received from £80 to £400 for Fashion Week shows. They also can often have terrible working conditions, with models rushing from show to show where their hair is backcombed into wacky styles and their make-up is done, often with dirty brushes due to the many models that have been there before them. Models rarely receive private changing areas and I have often experienced photographers taking my picture as I undress backstage, which is completely disgusting.

Backstage is often like a zoo. Usually present backstage are designers, photographers, stylists, dressers, make-up artists, hairstylists, journalists and anybody else who wants to be around. Designers often have agreements with beauty brands to sell the backstage images for promotional material, which the models are very rarely informed about yet required to model for. Models are lost in the craziness and often find out about their outfits a few minutes before the show, which can be problematic if the clothes are inappropriate, such as see-through, and the model does not feel comfortable in speaking up and making a fuss so soon before the start of a show.

There are also several types of shows. Some may involve models walking down a runway, whereas others (often called 'presentations') may require models to stand completely still for many hours. I have been in many presentations and had to stand for three to four hours while people came and inspected me, like a human statue. These can be very exhausting.

Nowadays, fashion shows are changing. Whereas the low rate of pay once reflected the 'usage' (see 'L is for Legal') of the job, as in the fact that a limited number of people would see the model and their images would supposedly not be used outside of the show, today with social media, brands can use fashion shows in many ways. They can sell the clothes models are wearing directly on social media as they walk down the runway ('click to buy') and use the images taken of models for their online presence, meaning they may not even have to shoot the clothes separately. While the value of models walking in fashion shows has increased dramatically, the rate of pay has fallen, if anything, due to the oversupply of models.

Despite the difficulties facing runway models, there is a reason it is such a competitive area of modelling: walking in the right show could launch your career and it is a very fun, exciting job, involving travel and working with the best designers all over the world. It is just important that you have all of the facts in order to decide whether this is right for you. As we will see in the next chapter, you should always feel empowered to make your own choices about your own career.

Anti-exploitation tips

- Decide whether you want to be a runway model. Just because you can doesn't necessarily mean that you should – I fit the requirements however choose not to do Fashion Week because of the stress involved!
- If you don't fit the requirements, don't put yourself through needless stress. If you are 5'8", understand that you will experience rejection for shows 99% of the time. Your agency may try to send you to Fashion Week castings in case you happen to book something, but understand the hard work required and reality of the process.
- Never be pressured into paying for someone to teach you how to walk. Your agency should help you for free if it is something they want you to improve upon.
- Watch for any extra costs associated with doing Fashion Week, such as extra composite cards – always ask your agency

beforehand of any expenses involved and ask them not to use your account. See 'E is for Expenses'.

- Prioritise your 'request' castings (see 'C is for Castings'). I tend to leave any castings with a queue of over an hour, as I weigh up my chances of success upon arrival. Remember that your agency often will send new castings throughout the day during Fashion Week so always keep your phone fully charged up.

- Remember that you can say no – to castings, shows or to Fashion Week itself. The process is extremely stressful and you don't have to do anything you don't want to do.

- Always request a private changing room at fashion shows and don't do anything that makes you feel uncomfortable, such as wearing a see-through outfit. If you have an issue, call your agency and tell the client as soon as possible.

- Models will often have people dressing them at fashion shows. Ensure that you feel comfortable with your dresser and remember that you can say no to having one at all if you wish.

- Try on the shoes you are expected to wear before walking in the show to ensure you feel safe and confident in them. Models are often given shoes that are too small or too high, so if you feel unsafe tell the client immediately. I was once expected to walk in eight-inch heels down a wet runway with strobe lighting – no joke! See 'D is for Danger'.

- If anybody wants to take your photograph backstage, ask them for a card and how they wish to use the images. Do not allow anyone to take your photograph unless you feel 100% comfortable, and if you have any issues with strangers backstage tell the client or your agency.

- Remember to stand up for yourself at fashion shows and not to give in to the fast-paced pressure. See 'Q is for Questions' for tips on how to do this.

- Avoid doing shows that are unpaid or very badly paid. It is usually a lot of stress for not much gain, and you may even be unrecognisable in the show anyway!

- Ensure that you ask for regular breaks, food and basic respect whenever you are working at a show. See 'K is for Knowing What to Expect'.

is for X-Rated

MANY MODELS FEEL like they don't have ownership of their own body. Daily requests by strangers to strip down to their underwear, change in public and pose nude are sadly commonly accepted as a normal part of the job. Models often do not realise the full implications that this can have on them and their lives, as they tend to be very young and naive, particularly at the start of their careers. Models and other professionals become desensitised to nudity, which can become very dangerous as it is forgotten that these models are often vulnerable human beings.

As seen in 'S is for Sexual Exploitation', many models suffer sexual harassment as a routine part of their job and exploitation for the sexual pleasure of others. Much of this is focused on nudity, due to the vulnerable position that many models find themselves in where they may be asked to show more of their body than they feel comfortable with. In this chapter, I will explain how this can happen in more detail, because it is such a common occurrence for models – and how they can reclaim ownership of their bodies and protect themselves

Did you know?

1. Models are often asked to undress in front of strangers and are often not provided with changing rooms on jobs.

2. Compromising images of models may be used against them for the rest of their lives. There is no way of knowing an image has been deleted and many photographers believe they own the images that they take, even if they don't.

3. Of models surveyed, 86.8% had been asked to change nude at a job or casting without advance notice; 27.5% of those posed nude because they felt they had to, even though they didn't want to.[63]

4. Many jobs will involve lingerie or nudity without the model being informed beforehand.

How are models exploited via nudity?

As models' bodies are essentially their work, they may be manipulated into taking nude images that will follow them around for the rest of their life. This starts with becoming a model – there are many fraudulent people who will manipulate aspiring models into sending nude images in the hope of becoming a model, which can be used to blackmail them. Legitimate agencies will never ask for partially or fully nude images. Once these images have been taken, they will exist forever.

Legitimate agencies should treat people with respect and ask them to take photographs in swimwear only once they have been signed, and if they feel comfortable. An agency will always own

---

[63] The Model Alliance, '2012 Industry Survey, Industry Analysis'. http://modelalliance.org/industry-analysis

these images, which should only be used to show the body of a model. They are often on the agency website as 'polaroids' and should always be extremely professional and not sexual in any way whatsoever, plain and non-suggestive. However, it can still be a dehumanising process to have your photograph taken essentially in your underwear and have your body scrutinised by strangers in the process. Models often sit around their model agencies in underwear waiting for bookers to finish their work and take their photographs. Female models often have to walk through offices of people in underwear and heels. This is not something a young, vulnerable person should be doing but is very common practice.

Male models are usually expected to have absolutely no problem being in underwear and can be laughed at if they do. It is forgotten that these are often young boys, who feel as insecure about their bodies as girls do and face the same issues getting undressed in front of strangers.

Model agencies theoretically should ensure that checks are in place for any modelling jobs involving nudity, swimwear or lingerie, including that the model has been fully informed and has given proper consent. They should check that the client is legitimate and is taking the photographs for a proper reason as opposed to private use!

Sadly, many models turn up to jobs and find out that they involve shooting partially clothed without being informed, which is sometimes the client's and sometimes the booker's fault. Regardless of the situation, models are often so desperate to do a good job that they are easily manipulated into believing their agency agreed to it and then made to feel that they are overreacting if they feel uncomfortable. They are made to feel like they need a reason to not want to shoot swimwear – my reason was studying law, but I have seen other models use religion and their parents as reasons. No one should need a reason not to do something they don't want to do. I have been made to feel like I am overreacting or being ridiculous for saying no to shooting underwear when I knew it would impact me being able to become a lawyer in the future.

If a model feels uncomfortable shooting, they are at risk because the perpetrator may try to 'relax' them or make them feel insecure about making a fuss. They are relaxed through being eased into it or by assurances such as that nipples will be edited out or nothing will be done with the images. However, these are strangers with their own interests at heart. I have seen many photographers sell images of models shot in underwear when they achieve later success, which have been printed in trashy newspapers and made to look as though the model shot them recently, when they were shot years ago! There is not much models can do about this and no way to ensure they follow through on their promises.

Ironically, it is the unpaid jobs where these situations happen the most – in test shoots that have not been properly checked out by the agency, as seen in 'B is for Book'. The amateurs involved in these shoots often do not know how to act professionally and could profit off the images, so may have motives that have little to do with fashion. Most of the worst situations I have encountered I have not even been paid for, not even with a proper client. On one particularly horrendous shoot I was made to dress up as a man in a suit when I said no to shooting lingerie, and was then pressured to spank another model with a pingpong bat for the entire day! In the end they 'covered my face' with my hair as I awkwardly clambered onto the pingpong table over the other model, crying under the safety of my hair. A model doesn't have to be naked to feel violated.

How can models deal with this pressure?

If you find yourself in a situation where you are being pressured to do something you don't want to do when you have already said no, leave. Put yourself first – it doesn't matter if you are being paid or not, no one has a legitimate reason to make you shoot partially clothed; nothing is more important than how you feel. Models are often seen as disposable, they come and they go, but they are the ones who will have to live with the consequences of their actions. It is important to speak to your agency as soon as possible if you feel uncomfortable on a job, which should support you but may not if it doesn't have your best interests at heart. I left an agency which told me off for not wanting to shoot a lingerie campaign because I finally realised they saw me as nothing more than a product. Some agencies will value and respect your wishes much more than others and it is important to be represented by an agency that stands up for you.

Models should discuss with their agency how they feel about nudity, swimwear and lingerie and know it is something they never have to do if they don't want to. I would highly advise any model to avoid shooting this if you can, because the images will be on the internet for everyone to see, for the rest of your life. Even seemingly legitimate work such as e-commerce can still involve you being pressured to shoot thongs and see-through underwear that makes you feel uncomfortable and can be viewed as overtly sexual imagery.

You have no idea what you may want to do in the future and topless or sexual images that appear in an online search of your name can block off many different professional careers.

Even if you are not shooting nudity, you may still encounter issues while changing on jobs. If a model is expected to change in public as is common industry practice, strangers may easily photograph them. This is particularly so in dangerous private situations where there may be hidden cameras, such as in a photographer's bedroom. It is important that models are vigilant about where they change and who they change in front of. They need to protect their body, as any other human would. As seen in 'W is for Walk', at Fashion Week it is very common to see professional photographers shooting models changing backstage, which would cause outcry if it was a group of producers or photographers themselves getting changed!

Models should always be given the choice as to where and how they change and should never be forced into being dressed by anyone. You are old enough to be self-employed, so you are old enough to be trusted to get dressed without destroying clothes. By taking back control of your personal space, you can give people permission to touch you in a certain way – whether that is tying your shoelaces or applying moisturiser to your chest – and empower yourself as a result. If someone does not ask your permission to touch you, ask them to stop. They will likely be very embarrassed and not even realise what they were doing – other professionals in the industry are often as desensitised to concepts of nudity and personal space as the models are.

Every situation is a balancing act, but by understanding the sanctity of your body and your power to say no, you can make informed decisions instead of letting people treat your body as theirs. This may often involve deciding whether someone is being rude or abusive, accidentally careless or intentionally exploitative, cruel or stupid. By calling them out on their actions, simply saying, 'I don't feel comfortable', you are showing that you understand how you should be treated.

As we will see in the next chapter, it is important for models to look at their careers and lives as a whole instead of living in the moment. They are not disposable and have many broader career opportunities waiting ahead of them.

Anti-exploitation tips

- If you feel unsafe, leave.
- If you feel uncomfortable, call your agent. Go to the bathroom and give them a quick call, they will advise you on what to do. Always trust your own gut instinct and if you don't agree with their advice, follow your own instinct.
- Never do anything that you may later regret. If you want to go into a career such as law or the civil service, establish boundaries on the types of jobs you are willing to do. Always consider whether it is worth doing something you

are uncomfortable with to please a stranger or for a certain amount of money, if that is going to restrict you later in life.

- Always tell a client when you arrive to a job if you do not feel comfortable with anything.
- If a client is rude to you, ask them to stop. Clients often don't even realise that they are being rude, and a gentle, polite reminder will shock them into treating you with the respect you deserve. All it takes is a 'Excuse me, some of the things you are saying such as (X) / the way you are treating me is upsetting me, could you please be a bit more mindful? I am doing my best'.
- If someone is pressuring you into doing something you don't want to do, such as trying to kiss you or take your phone number, say NO. 'Sorry but I don't feel comfortable with that', is all you need to say.
- Never give anyone your phone number if you don't want to.
- Never send anyone you don't know any images of you online.
- Avoid potentially dangerous situations by assessing them first. Sometimes agents make mistakes and can send you to clients they haven't fully checked out, so do your research on every client before doing the job. If a shoot is at a photographer's house, be cautious.
- Always tell someone else where you are going, such as a friend or relative. Drop them the address and what time you should be finished.
- Always request a private changing room on castings and jobs.

is for Your Career

I‍T IS OFTEN assumed that models' careers end very quickly, and while some do, some continue modelling all the way through their lives. Others use modelling as a stepping stone to other careers, as the experience you can gain as a model is very valuable to have on a CV. Modelling provides unique life opportunities where a lot of different skills are used on a daily basis.

Unfortunately, this is something that is often forgotten and models can develop serious anxieties as a result of believing modelling is their only opportunity for success in life, as seen in 'Z is for Zen'. It can become your entire identity, especially if you have no higher education qualifications, which becomes very problematic if you are unhappy in the job.

In this chapter, I will demonstrate how to leave the industry, figure out what to do next and build a strong CV in order to transfer to other career routes smoothly and confidently. By being objective about your career and viewing the larger picture, you can feel empowered to always make the best decisions for yourself.

Did you know?

1. Models are self-employed and many have effectively run their own businesses since their teenage years.

2. Models can decide their own schedules and book out certain periods of time or days, meaning it can be easy to try out different internships alongside modelling.

3. Many models are pressurised to leave school or university in order to pursue modelling and feel as though they have no 'back-up' career.

How to build your career

1. Establish who you are outside of modelling.

    By understanding your personal identity, figuring out what your values are and what makes you happy, you can plan your career effectively. Modelling is great because it is so flexible – you can easily work on the side and gain experience in different areas without being tied to internships and jobs.

    Tips for this include the following.
    o Write down everything that you are passionate about. Start learning about it – read books, watch lectures and speak to people working in those areas.
    o Gain experience in the industry, especially if you have any personal connections. Dedicate one or two days per week, no matter what modelling jobs come up, and ensure it is paid.
    o Formally educate yourself if you can – modelling is great to do on the side of university.
    o Have a side job in anything at all – this will provide you with experience and a stable income. Many companies such as fashion stores specifically hire models and have flexible hours.

o Start a blog – this is great to practise using your voice and to share with others what inspires you. It is a great addition to a CV and a document of your life.
o Volunteer – helping others in need is a great way to learn what you are passionate about and give back to society.

2. Write your CV.

Models have a lot of great skills that are applicable to other jobs – they are self-employed and have much more life experience than the typical 20-something, often with international travel, self-management and experience working with huge brands. Keep your CV constantly updated and ready to send out to jobs that appeal to you.

CV tips for models include the following.
o Keep it simple and to one page, with concise information backed up by specific examples, such as 'professionalism', and give specific examples of this (e.g., 'working with the editor of a fashion magazine').
o Highlight your best moments, such as the most prominent companies you have worked for. Employers will find it a welcome change to read unique experiences of the modelling world and understand how they are applicable to their career.
o Keep it relevant by editing your CV for each job you apply for, ensuring all the grammar is perfect. Always write a great cover letter showing you are serious about the position you are applying for.

Skills models may list on their CV include the following.
o Self-management. As a self-employed model, you effectively set up your own business and run your own career, which includes everything from choosing your agency to managing your jobs. This is very valuable, especially from a young age, as it proves that you can organise and motivate yourself to work.

○ Financial skills, including working with numbers, sending invoices, filing tax returns and budgeting. Your agency may manage most of your invoices and payments; however, you as the model are responsible for ensuring that you get paid, invoicing your agency, filing a tax return, saving your tax each year, budgeting off sporadic and ever-changing payments, dealing with international payments, assessing how much commission has been taken from your payments and understanding what it all means. A model has to keep track of all of their outstanding payments often on a global scale, in different currencies. You essentially are your own book-keeper and accountant, even if you employ one to help you with your finances. These skills are a vital part of any job, but especially relevant to jobs involving organisation and administration, such as being a personal assistant or secretary.

○ Marketing, especially social media. Models market themselves every day to clients in castings and online via social media. They understand the back end of an image and what goes into advertising campaigns.

○ Punctuality and organisation. Models must always be on time, and are adept at managing their own schedule, which may often have clashing castings and jobs and be in foreign cities. They become excellent at preparation and time-keeping.

○ Great under pressure and excellent interpersonal skills. Models have to maintain a polite demeanour, look beautiful and smile even when they are exhausted after shooting for 12 hours in the freezing cold. They are confident mastering 150 outfit changes and maintain professionalism even while being prodded and poked in the midst of a high-pressure photoshoot, where all of the focus is on them. These skills are great for jobs such as retail, customer service and high-pressured businesses in particular.

○ Teamwork. Models are excellent at meeting, bonding and working with complete strangers. Each job involves a different team of strangers, who may not even speak the same language as the model yet they all manage to work together for the same goal. Teamwork is an essential part of any job.

○ Sales. Models have had to sell everything from body paint to shoulder pads. They are adept at bringing products to life, understanding them and showcasing them in the best light. Models also have to sell themselves at every casting they attend, in what essentially are sales pitches to the client.

○ Networking. Models have to mingle and be presentable to anyone from heads of fashion powerhouses to world-famous celebrities. They have to build strong connections with complete strangers in order to maintain a successful career. This is useful for any career but especially business-related ones.

○ Creativity. Modelling is a creative job, and requires a lot of outside-of-the-box thinking for instructions such as, 'look angry but with a happy twinkle in your eye', bringing images to life and working with other creatives.

○ Adaptability. The ability to listen to what the client wants and apply themselves, whether that is waiting for three hours for a casting or performing a script to a room full of strangers. Models tend to find out the details of a shoot at the very last minute and therefore have to be able to adapt to any situation and any people. Models can be sent to a country where they don't speak the language and expected to begin working three jobs per day. They have to listen to what their agent and client want from them and be obedient and attentive, while maintaining their own boundaries. This is a great life skill, as it means models are generally better at coping than other people of their age with unpredictable situations and change.

○ Acting. Models often pick up acting skills in their careers, which can also lead to opportunities in presenting, public speaking and events.

3. Understand what you want from modelling and how it can help you.

Modelling is great to do alongside a variety of internships and can help you gain international experience before you are ready to fully commit to a career. By figuring out what your goals are with modelling, you can ensure you achieve these before moving on to a more stable job and are less tempted to return – think of it like a bucket list! Remember to save your money and avoid getting into debt to make the most of modelling, so that you can sustain yourself through quieter periods.

4. When you are truly ready to change career, leave your agency.

It is important to leave your agency so that you do not get tempted back into modelling, and make a proper commitment to your new job. By not having emails pop into your inbox as you sit in your cold office cubicle offering you a photoshoot in Mexico next week, you will be less tempted to return to modelling instead of focusing on your long-term career. It is very hard to have one foot in modelling and one foot in a stable job you want to succeed in. All careers require hard work and will have downsides – it's important to remind yourself of the reasons modelling is not for you by having a list to hand!

Leaving an agency is not usually an issue if a model is leaving the industry completely. However, contracts are legally binding and every situation involves careful consideration, especially if you are leaving one agency for another. See 'L is for Legal' on understanding your agency contract. Tips on this include the following.

○ Speak to your agency honestly and in person about why you want to leave them. They will probably agree to have you back whenever you want to return!

○ Check for any contractual restrictions such as minimum terms (stating that you must model for a certain period of time – always a red flag) or notice periods (that can often be around three months). Generally, an agency will not bind you to this if you wish to change career completely, and even if you wish to change model agency it is unlikely that they will legally hold you to this unless they have a good reason to.

○ Check for any debt you may be in and discuss with your agency the best way to proceed. Some may not force you to repay this, especially if the debt is from overseas, you were not told about it or were pressured to accept; however, it depends on the amount and the agency. If you are made to repay it you can figure out a payment plan with your agency, always consulting with your union for help.

○ Remember to regularly check in with your agency every few months to check for any new payments from existing jobs.

Modelling can provide incredible opportunities to discover yourself and what you want from life. You can take charge of the flexible hours and empower yourself to make decisions that suit your life in general, making the industry work for you instead of being a victim to it. As we will see in the next chapter, many models do not empower themselves in this way and suffer with their mental health as they desperately try to cling onto the rollercoaster that modelling can be, instead of taking charge of the steering wheel.

is for Zen

WORKING AS A model can often feel like being someone else's doll. You bring other people's visions to reality, with your life permanently held in someone else's hands. As a result of the constant change and unstable lifestyle models encounter, many do not have a clear image of who they are.

It is hard to find a sense of control over your life when other people decide where you should live, when you will be paid and what jobs you will be doing. Maintaining friendships, hobbies and interests when your entire life is available for booking and strangers are able to rent you out for the day is also incredibly difficult. It is hardly surprising that with so much exploitation and so little protection available for models, many suffer from serious mental health issues.

In this chapter, I will demonstrate how models can take charge of their mental health and establish firm personal boundaries to protect themselves.

Did you know?

1. Many models suffer with mental health issues. One survey found that 68.3% of surveyed models suffer from anxiety and/or depression, 31.2% have had eating disorders and 50.6% had been exposed to cocaine.[64]

2. It is very difficult for models to take holidays and proper breaks from work, because they can be called to work at any time. Due to the scarcity of jobs, it is very troublesome for a model to even have a sick day if they are unwell.

3. Many models suffer from a lack of routine or stability, due to having such an unpredictable life.

Mental illnesses

Some of the mental struggles that models may encounter as a result of the industry include the following.

*   Depression.

    Feelings of hopelessness and sadness that last several days can amount to depression. Many models may experience this in forms of low self-worth, low self-esteem and low enjoyment due to the stresses and exploitation they face, not working and feeling trapped in the industry, especially if they don't have a strong identity outside of modelling.

*   Anxiety.

    Feelings of constant worry and stress can amount to anxiety, which can be crippling. There are several forms of anxiety that may revolve around having to do certain things, being around people or having panic attacks. Many models have anxiety due to the constant fear of not working again and

---

64 The Model Alliance, '2012 Industry Survey, Industry Analysis'. http://modelalliance.org/industry-analysis

never feeling good enough, as their self-worth often stems from the opinions of others.

- Eating disorders.

As seen in 'M is for Measurements', many models suffer from eating disorders such as anorexia, bulimia and over-exercising due to the pressure to look a certain way.

- Body dysmorphic disorder.

Many models believe that they look a certain way that is completely different to reality. This is due to being pressured to fit into unrealistic measurements, a world away from normal society.

- Addictions and substance abuse.

Many models suffer addictions to smoking, alcohol and drugs because of stress, lack of routine and often being offered these for free when they are young and vulnerable. These can result in very serious illnesses and destroy lives.

If you are suffering with any of these or anything else that is causing you stress, please see a doctor, who can help you. Do not suffer needlessly.

Practising self-love and mindfulness

The best way for us all to deal with the craziness of life is to be a little kinder to ourselves, spend more time figuring out what makes us happy and do it! This is all that mindfulness and self-love involves, putting yourself first and respecting yourself as you would any person you really love.

We have to choose to be happy every single minute of every single day, whether that is from the thoughts we are having or the people we are spending time with.

Self-love can come in various forms, including the following.

1. Take a holiday.

    Models often find it hard to take a holiday or book days off work, because of the fear that jobs will come up when they are away. Dedicate some time to yourself each month where you know you will have the day off and spend the day doing exactly what you enjoy, figuring out what makes you happy, without the pressure to see anybody else. Take a holiday without turning it into a work trip by finding photographers to shoot and seeing agencies. Don't have the pressure of being 'accepted' by anyone for a week or two.

2. Learn how to enjoy spending time with yourself.

    Set yourself a fun goal for each week that you can do in your spare time, such as visiting a museum or doing a dance class. Write down all of the things that you enjoy doing and make a bucket list of things to try – anything from reading a book about Chinese history to finger painting. Clearly define to yourself what you enjoy doing and what makes you happy, and make sure you do it whenever you are feeling sad.

3. Exercise.

    This will boost your endorphins and get your blood and focus flowing out of your mind and into your body. My favourite exercises to do include yoga and dancing. They never fail to make me feel happy and I always try to go to a couple of classes each week or do them in my bedroom at home.

4. Reconnect with your body.

    As humans, we can be pretty mean to our bodies. By writing down three things you like about how you look every morning, you can begin to reconnect and appreciate how beautiful you are on the outside as well as the inside. Catch yourself saying anything negative about yourself and make an effort to only think positively about yourself.

5. Choose the people in your life carefully.

Many models are incredibly lonely due to the nature of their job and so can often have toxic friends and relationships. By thinking about how these people make you feel and identifying any potentially abusive characteristics like control or manipulation you can eliminate toxic people. Choose your friends based on sharing common values and spend healthy time together without alcohol being involved. Remember to check in with the people who love you such as your family every day, and maintain these relationships despite the instability of your routine.

6. Meditate.

Meditation is different for everybody. There is no right or wrong way to do it – you don't have to sit for an hour with no thoughts, you can have a clear mind or a racing mind, you can focus on the breath swooping into your lungs or you can focus on a mantra that you repeat in your mind. You can sit with a straight back with index finger and thumb touching or you can go for a run. For me, meditation is just about taking a couple of minutes per day to take a deep breath.

I believe that meditation is simply focusing on the nice feeling you have inside your chest – just breathing normally. If you try now, you will be able to feel it too. Just concentrate on a tingling sensation inside your chest. That is who 'you' are. You are not your thoughts, you are the one listening to them. You do not have to engage with them and act upon them.

7. Have a routine.

By having a routine that is the same every day, you are able to build stability into your life no matter what. This can be a morning or night routine, involving anything from stretching to journalling, speaking to someone you love or simply having a shower. I do yoga every morning as soon as I wake up and write in my diary before doing anything else.

8. Practise gratitude.

   Write down all of the things that make you smile every day
   – from old people holding hands to a dog in the park. Once
   you realise how amazing the world around you is, it becomes
   quite hard to stay wrapped up in your own mind! See 'G is for
   Gratitude' for more.

9. Do grounding exercises to bring yourself into the present.

   When I get very stressed out I try to notice all of the things
   around me, such as all of the different shades of green I can
   see. This distracts my brain from worrying and helps me to
   focus on the present moment. The past already happened
   and the future is going to happen regardless of what we think
   now, so we may as well just focus on the now.

10. See a therapist once a month.

    I strongly believe that all models should regularly see a
    therapist. Many therapists work via Skype and cost the
    same price as a night out, yet are so much better for you.
    It is simply someone to listen to your worries and give you
    some objective advice, forming part of a healthy routine and
    support network.

11. Limit your screen time.

    Social media can be a very depressing thing for models, who
    face pressure to have a strong online presence (as seen in 'I is
    for Instagram') and so can spend unhealthy amounts of time
    online comparing themselves to others' filtered highlights of
    their life. I advise having a phone-free first and last hour of
    your day, as social media can become very addictive and send
    you in a downward spiral.

12. Re-train your brain.

    It is very helpful to notice how you are thinking and why,
    choosing new thoughts. We all have stories playing out in
    our minds that we are the star of, and it's helpful to notice

negative thinking patterns we may have so we can change them. Whenever I find myself thinking a negative thought, I ask myself the following.

○ Where has this thought come from? What has triggered it? I especially look behind that to the real reason. For example, I often worry about someone not liking me, which is linked to being bullied as a child.

○ Can I find proof that this thought is not true? For example, as I can't read minds there is no way to tell if someone doesn't like me.

○ What is this thought doing to me? Usually, if I think someone doesn't like me I will stress out about it for hours, subconsciously disliking them in the process!

○ Can I prove the opposite is true? For example, if they have invited me out for a coffee.

It is okay not to be okay. Remember that you are perfect, exactly how you are. Please seek help if you are suffering and remember that modelling is an enormously stressful job that involves things no one should have to go through. Be kind to yourself and watch out for those around you, from your family to strangers on the train.

The world can be a tough place for us all, and always can do with a little more kindness, laughter and smiles.

Conclusion

*T*HE *MODEL MANIFESTO* has hopefully shone a light on the exploitative practices that models undergo every day as a routine part of their jobs. Demystifying the smoke-and-mirrors of the industry allows us to objectively consider it for what it is: young, vulnerable people working in adult careers, often with an extremely limited say in their own lives. It becomes much easier to empathise with these beautiful creatures when we recognise that they do not naturally spring out of bed looking like they do in the magazines – much hard work, dedication and exploitation goes into the image portrayed to society.

Modelling has certainly given me once-in-a-lifetime experiences and enabled me to live a life filled with adventure, but these adventures have mostly been at the mercy of other people. The trick to having a successful, happy career as a model is education – by understanding what the job entails, you can make conscious decisions about your career and choose the course of your life. Knowledge is power – by learning all of the information in this book, you will be much better equipped to face the industry as an empowered, strong model.

The time has come for models to come together and demand better working conditions. This book is a call to action for you not only to empower yourself but those around you, to use your voice and speak out about the injustices you may face in your life. For too long, models have been treated like silent mannequins, degraded in the name of beauty and exploited because they are simply lucky to be a model in the first place. They deserve the same regulation and protection as any other industry, humane treatment and basic respect. This may be the end of the book, but it is only the beginning of the campaign.

Find out about how you can become more involved at www.themodelmanifesto.com.

Manifesto for Change:
A Call to Action

A SPIRING AND CURRENT models are severely exploited on a daily basis all over the world. With no minimum age to model in the UK, many start while under the age of 18. Children are working in fully fledged, adult careers as a result – running their own business in the eyes of the law!

Models sign over their legal capacity to model agents, yet remain fully legally liable themselves. Untrained strangers hold their entire lives in their hands, with the ability to sign contracts and spend money on their behalf, even sending them to live across the world, with no accountability to the model at all. Contrastingly, aspiring models are paying thousands of pounds every day to fraudulent model agencies in the hope of becoming signed.

Self-regulation of the fashion industry clearly does not work, as identified by the extensive, very troubling issues concerning models discussed in this book. Codes of conduct lack proper enforcement procedures and are often established by those directly profiting from models. Even with proper education, models are still being lured into exploitative contracts as the industry is so uniquely glamourised and unregulated.

This is a call to the government to step in, to protect vulnerable people who do not possess real capacity to enter into a profession where their bodies will be traded. To protect those who are manipulated into signing unfair contracts, enslaved to exploitative agencies and trafficked around the world to pay off their debts. The children who have no protection by virtue of being 'self-employed' yet cannot even have a sick day from work without being held legally liable. This manifesto is a call to agents to honour their duty of care to their models and act in a transparent, respectful and collaborative manner. It is a call to clients to honour their duty of care to models in the workplace and to provide them with safe, respectful working environments. It is a call to models to honour their responsibilities to those they work with and, most importantly, themselves. Last but not least, this is a call to society who glamorises the modelling industry and holds it up on a pedestal.

By doing the below, the government can acknowledge the unique status of fashion models to protect thousands of people.

- Setting a minimum age to join a model agency in any capacity.
- Setting a standard maximum total rate of agency commission in the UK, to be public knowledge.
- Requiring UK model agencies to have a government-provided licence to operate, with those licensed listed publicly online.
- Enforcing membership of an official trade union for models.
- Reviewing the employment status of models.

Glossary

A

- Account. A financial account a model has with their agency that keeps track of money the agency has spent on the model's behalf. This will be repaid to the agency as the model earns money.
- Advance. When an agency pays money on a model's behalf, occasionally referring to paying them money before the client has paid. They may charge an 'advance fee' for this, which is a charge to the model and may increase over time. An agency will need a financial licence to charge this.
- Age category. The age range within which a model appears to be.
- Agency. The company that looks after models and books them work. The people who work in an agency are called agents or bookers.
- Angles. The most photogenic angles of a model's face.

B

- Backstage. The area behind a catwalk where models get ready.
- Beauty. Focusing on a model's face.
- Behind-the-scenes/BTS. Usually refers to unofficial footage shot during a modelling job.
- Billing form. A form used by models to record their hours of work, often seen abroad.
- Book. A model's portfolio of images to show to clients.
- Booker. A person working in a modelling agency who books work for models.
- Booking form. The form an agency and client signs with all of the terms and conditions of a specific job.

- Book out. Notification to an agent that a model is not available for work.
- Buy-out. Payment for the extra use of images featuring the model, often after a job has been completed.
- Boutique agency. An agency with a small number of models, often focused on a specific genre.

C

- Call time. The time at which a model must be at a job and ready to work.
- Call-back/recall. A second casting with shortlisted models.
- Campaigns. Shoots that summarise and promote a client's collection, normally in a few pictures.
- Cancellation. When one party cancels a confirmed booking. Because of the high production costs involved in planning shoots, a doctor's note is normally required if a model wishes to cancel a job due to illness.
- Casting. When a model meets a client with the aim of booking work.
- Casting agency. Agencies specialised in casting models for clients.
- Casting brief/call. The information the agency receives for a casting, detailing the type of model the client is looking for and the job.
- Casting director. The person responsible for organising castings, who may select models from a casting to put forward to the client for final selection.
- Casting video. When they're considering a model for a job, a client can request a video of that model introducing themselves and showing some poses and their personality.
- Catalogue. Printed booklets showing a client's collections.
- Catwalk/runway. The narrow, elevated platform that models walk across to show clothing during a fashion show.
- Chart. A model's schedule that their agency manages, showing their options and upcoming jobs. They can 'check their chart' by speaking to their bookers.
- Chicken fillets/cutlets. Pieces of squishy plastic that give models padding, normally placed in their underwear.

- Classic model. A model usually used to market to an older audience, generally over the age of 35.
- Client. The party that pays the model.
- Close-up. A tight frame of a person or object.
- Commercial modelling. Everything that isn't associated with high fashion, such as product advertisements.
- Come off. When an option has been declined by a client, this is often referred to as having 'come off' or having been 'released'.
- Contact sheet. A sheet developed by a photographer showing all the 'selects' (selected images) on a job to see the general mood.
- Collaborations. Often referring to when a model and a client work together for free or for something other than money, such as clothes. Most commonly seen with social media.
- Composite card. A piece of card printed with at least two photos of the model and their details to give to clients.
- Confidentiality agreement. Often seen on jobs involving celebrities or unreleased collections stating that models legally cannot disclose or share any information or pictures about the job to anyone at all outside of the job.
- Confirmation. When a model has been booked on a job.
- Copyright. The ownership of images, which models rarely have. This means that they usually need permission from the client or photographer to use their own pictures in another commercial setting that makes them money.
- Cover shoot. A photoshoot for the cover of a publication.
- Creative director. The person who has put the job together.
- Curve. Refers to plus-sized modelling.

D

- Daily schedule. Detailing a model's appointments or bookings, which they receive the night before.
- Day rate. The amount a model will be paid for a day's work.
- Digitals. Also known as 'digis' or 'polaroids', these are the pictures an agency will take of a model to show how they naturally look.

- Direct. Booking a job with a client directly, without the use of an agency.
- Direct booking. The model may not have met the client beforehand in a casting before being booked on a job, often for foreign clients.
- Dresser. Someone who helps models get dressed, mainly to protect the clothes. Usually seen at fashion shows when models have to change quickly.

E

- Editorial. A magazine photoshoot, often playing out a 'story'.
- E-commerce. The sale of goods directly from an image on a website, usually referring to online fashion brands.
- Exclusivity. The right of a client to use a model in a certain category for a given period of time in given countries whereby no competitive brand can use that model.

F

- Fitting. Usually unpaid sessions that take place prior to a job where the clothes to be modelled are 'fitted' on to the model.
- Fitting job. A paid session where a designer makes the clothes on the model, who is often a 'fit model' with specific measurements.
- Fashion Week. When top designers show their collections over a few days. Most countries have their own Fashion Week.
- Full day. Usually six to eight hours of work (9am–6pm is standard) where a day rate is charged.
- Full-length. A photograph focusing on a model's entire body.

G

- Go-see. An informal meeting between a client and model for future work but with no specific job in mind.
- General casting. When the client has not requested to see any specific models, usually meaning there will be long queues.

Models are not strictly required to attend these by their agency. They may also be called 'cattle calls' or 'open call' castings.

H

- Half-day. One to six hours of work, where a half-day rate is charged and lunch is not provided.
- Hair jobs. Jobs involving cutting, colouring and styling hair.
- Hair and make-up (H&M). A hair and make-up job.
- Hair stylist. The hairdresser who styles a model's hair on a job.
- Hero shot. The most important shot of the job, which will be used as the main feature image.
- High fashion. Highly esteemed fashion work involving top designers and publications.

I

- Influencer model. A model with the ability to influence a large number of people with their social media following and therefore commandeer higher rates of pay.
- Image board. Often referred to as the high-fashion division of a model agency.
- Image job. Work requiring models to portray a certain 'image', usually at an event.

J

- Job. A paid booking for a model.

K

- Kit bag. What a model should take to a job as requested by the client.

L

- Lingerie. Underwear.
- Lighting. There are several types of lights used on photoshoots to ensure the model looks their best.
- Location shoot/'on location'. Usually means a job that is not in a studio, so it can be anywhere at all.
- Look-book. A printed 'book' featuring a designer's collection that buyers and customers can look through.
- Looks. The number of outfits or different looks (such as hair and make-up changes) a model will have during a job.

M

- Main board. An agency division where models are more established and experienced.
- Make-up artist. The person who will do a model's make-up for a job.
- Make-up scarf. What a model puts over their head while changing to ensure that make-up doesn't get on the clothes.
- Markets. The various geographical locations where models can earn a living.
- Maternity. Usually referring to shooting maternity clothes, regardless of whether a model is pregnant. They can be given a prosthetic belly to strap on.
- Mood board. Images that are used as inspiration for a job.
- Mother agent. A model's first agency, which takes a commission from all of their work and may contract them out to other agencies.

N

- Natural light. Refers to sunlight.
- New faces. An agency division representing models who are newer and less experienced than the other models.
- Nudity. Nudity on jobs can refer to simply being topless or 'full' nudity.

O

- On stay. When a model goes to another city or country for a period of anywhere between one and three months to work.
- Option. When a model is shortlisted for a job. These can usually be first, second, third or fourth options.

P

- Parts model. A model whose work focuses on a specific part of their body, such as their hands.
- Per-diem. Payment given to models by a client when travelling to cover their daily expenses. This can also be referred to as pocket money and is not required to be repaid to the client.
- Photographer. The person who is photographing the model.
- Plus-sized model. Usually a model of size 12/14 and above.
- Pocket money. Cash payments usually paid to foreign models on a weekly basis who cannot easily access their bank accounts and need money to survive. In this context the money is usually advanced by the agency and may be accompanied by interest fees.
- Poses. How models show the clothes as they are being photographed.
- Polaroids. Also known as 'digitals', these are very natural images of a model taken by their agency.
- Portrait. A photograph featuring on the upper half of a model.
- Prepared/'prepped'. Normally involves being prepared for lingerie/swimwear, ensuring that body hair is minimal.
- Presentation. Jobs involving presenting something on the model, whether it is a haircut/style, clothes, jewellery or make-up. They normally have a stage instead of a catwalk.
- Prints. Images that have been printed out onto high-quality paper to go into a model's portfolio.
- Profile. The way a model looks from the side.

- Promotional jobs. Promoting a product or service in a more commercial fashion, such as a car or a wedding fair.
- Promoters. People who may be paid to bring models to clubs or events.

R

- Rate. The rate of pay.
- Recognisable. When the model is recognisable in pictures taken on a shoot.
- Request casting. When a client requests to cast a specific model for a job.
- Royalties. The money a model receives as a result of their work being published or used for a longer amount of time or in a different way to previously agreed, possibly on a regular basis, such as yearly.
- Release form. Permission by the model to use their image in a certain way. These are often signed on behalf of the model by their agency for paid work.

S

- Scout. Someone who discovers models.
- Self-assessment. The tax declaration that models will have to submit at the end of each financial year.
- Set. The location of a shoot, usually the specific area where the model is being photographed.
- Showroom. Where a designer's collection is based, which can be used for private showings or appointments with buyers. They are not normally open to the public.
- Showroom model. A model who works in a showroom, wearing and sampling pieces of a collection to buyers and customers.

- Stylist. The person who puts outfits together and decides what the model wears.
- Studio. A room where photoshoots take place, usually involving a backdrop, lighting and photography equipment.
- Stats. The model's statistics, such as height, bust, waist, hips and shoe size.
- Submission. Shoots that are submitted to magazines for publication.

T

- Test. A shoot that a model does to build their portfolio.
- Tear sheet. A page from a magazine, catalogue or other print job featuring a model.
- Trade for prints. When no one is being paid on a shoot and are all building their portfolios.

U

- Usage. How the images or film will be used from a job, in terms of media, in which locations and for how long.
- Union. An entity that will protect the rights of a group of people who work in the same industry.

V

- Videographer. A person who is filming video on a job.

W

- Walk. A model's signature way of walking down a catwalk, usually in high heels.
- Weather day. Another day which has been optioned in case of bad weather on the planned date of the job.

Additional reading

For further resources including agency recommendations and guides following this book, go to www.themodelmanifesto.com. You can also follow us on Instagram @themodelmanifesto to keep up-to-date.

Activism

- 'Regulate the UK fashion modelling industry'. A petition to call the government to action and regulate the UK model industry.
  www.change.org/p/government-the-model-manifesto-ending-exploitation-by-education

- The hashtag #myjobshouldnotincludeabuse. Cameron Russell shared stories of abuse within the modelling industry using this; see 'Models are sharing their experiences with sexual assault via Instagram', *Refinery29*, 13 October 2017.   www.refinery29.com/en-us/2017/10/176509/cameron-russell-instagram-sexual-assault-stories

- 'Create a law to protect models from getting dangerously skinny!' Rosalie Nelson's petition to the government to outlaw dangerously skinny models.
  www.change.org/p/jackiedp-help-protect-models-from-getting-dangerously-skinny-rosalienelson-modelslaw-lfw

- Casting agent James Scully's revelations of the abusive practices at a top casting; see 'Supermodels back model mistreatment revelation', *Vogue*, 1 March 2017. www.vogue.co.uk/article/james-scully-model-mistreatment-post

Laws and regulations

- LVMH and Kering, 'The Charter on the Working Relations with Fashion Models and their Well-Being'. www.wecareformodels.com/wp-content/uploads/2018/01/The-Charter-on-fashion-models-LVMH-Kering-1p-EN.pdf
- Conde Naste Code of Conduct. www.condenastinternational.com/about-us/code-of-conduct/
- UK Government Regulations on fees that can be charged to models. www.gov.uk/entertainment-and-modelling-agencies/fees-for-fashion-and-photographic-models
- The Employment Agencies Act 1974. www.legislation.gov.uk/ukpga/1973/35
- The Conduct of Employment Agencies and Employment Businesses Regulations 2003. www.legislation.gov.uk/uksi/2003/3319/pdfs/uksi_20033319_en.pdf

Legal decisions

- Raske v Next Mgt., LLC. 2013 NY Slip Op 32103(U). A class action lawsuit of models suing top model agents in the USA. www.leagle.com/decision/innyco20130916214
- Decision of the Competition and Markets Authority, Case CE/9859-14. A decision against the Association of Model Agents (today the BFMA) with regards to price fixing. https://assets.publishing.service.gov.uk/media/58d8eb1840f0b606e7000030/modelling-sector-infringement-decision.pdf

Websites

- The Model Manifesto. www.themodelmanifesto.com/
- The British Fashion Model Agents Association. www.bfma.fashion/
- Equity. www.equity.org.uk/
- The Model Alliance. http://modelalliance.org/